# INDIA

## MICHAEL ALLABY

James Gillespies Primary
Whitehouse Loan
EDINBURGH
EH9 1BD

Evans

## TITLES IN THE COUNTRIES OF THE WORLD SERIES:

ARGENTINA • AUSTRALIA • BRAZIL • CANADA • CHINA
EGYPT • FRANCE • GERMANY • INDIA • ITALY • JAPAN
KENYA • MEXICO • NIGERIA • POLAND • UNITED KINGDOM
USA • VIETNAM

Published by Evans Brothers Limited
2A Portman Mansions
Chiltern Street
London W1U 6NR

**Reprinted 2006**

**British Library Cataloguing in Publication Data**
Allaby, Michael
India. – (Countries of the world)
1.India – Juvenile literature
I.Title
954'.053

ISBN 0 237 52755 3
13 - digit ISBN 978 0 237 52755 6

Editor: Daniel Rogers
Designer: Victoria Webb
Picture researchers: Lynda Lines and Frances Bailey
Map artwork by Peter Bull
Charts and graph artwork by Encompass Graphics Limited

Produced for Evans Brothers Limited by
Monkey Puzzle Media Limited
Gissing's Farm, Fressingfield
Suffolk IP21 5SH, UK

Picture acknowledgements
Photographs were taken by Mark Henley except for the following which were kindly supplied by: Corbis 10 bottom (David Samuel Robbins), 12 (Lindsay Hebberd), 16 top (Lindsay Hebberd), 16 bottom (Chris Lisle); Corbis Digital Stock front endpapers, 57; Eye Ubiquitous/Hutchison 13 bottom (David Brinicombe), 18 (Mary Jelliffe), 19 (Nick Haslam), 29 top (Patricio Goycoolea), 41 (Bennett Dean); Getty Images 52 top (Indranil Mukherjee); Link Picture Library 17 (DPL/Link India); MPM Images front cover upper middle, 27, 56 top; Reuters 13 top (Kamal Kishore), 21 (Sherwin Crasto), 22 (Sherwin Crasto), 22–23 (Utpal Barvah), 34 bottom (Pawel Kopczynski), 37 (Jayanta Shaw), 38 (Karamallah Daher), 39 bottom (Pawel Kopczynski), 51 bottom (Sherwin Crasto); Rex Features 50 (SIPA); Still Pictures 8 (Hartmut Schwarzbach), 9 (Anders Gunnartz), 14 (Shehzad Noorani), 15 top (Mark Edwards), 23 (Joerg Boethling), 26 bottom (Wolfgang Schmidt), 29 bottom (S Ganguly/UNEP), 31 top (Mark Edwards), 31 bottom (Ron Giling), 33 top (Mark Edwards), 33 bottom (Joerg Boethling), 35 (Singh/UNEP), 36 top (Johann Scheibner), 36 bottom (Sebastian Bolesch), 42 (Mark Edwards), 43, 45 (Mark Edwards), 46 (Hartmut Schwarzbach), 47 (Hoescht Marion Roussel), 48 right (Shehzad Noorani), 49 (Chris Martin), 52 bottom (Anders Gunnartz), 54 bottom (Mark Edwards), 55 (Fateh Singh Rathore), 56 bottom (Shehzad Noorani); Thirdangle.com front cover lower middle, 6–7, 10 top, 44 both, 61.
© copyright Evans Brothers 2005

**Endpapers (front):** The Taj Mahal at Agra, Uttar Pradesh, perhaps the world's most famous building.
**Title page:** A farmer in Orissa using oxen to plough his paddy field.
**Imprint and Contents pages:** Pushkar Lake, Rajasthan, with the city behind. Pushkar is a place of pilgrimage for Hindus.
**Endpapers (back):** A view of Mumbai from the sea.

# CONTENTS

INTRODUCING INDIA    8

INDIA'S LANDSCAPES    10

CLIMATE    18

POPULATION    24

GOVERNMENT    34

AGRICULTURE AND FORESTRY    40

INDUSTRY    46

TRANSPORT AND COMMUNICATIONS    52

THE ENVIRONMENT, LEISURE AND TOURISM    54

GLOSSARY    58

FURTHER INFORMATION    59

INDEX    60

The Indian flag consists of three bands: orange representing courage and sacrifice, white for purity and green for growth. The central wheel symbol, or chakra, signifies that in life there is movement.

Morning at Varanasi, when Hindus bathe ritually in the River Ganges.

India is the world's seventh-largest country and has the second-largest population. Its civilisation is one of the world's oldest and richest, stretching back for more than 4,000 years to a sophisticated culture that flourished in the Indus Valley. Today India combines ancient traditions with modern industries and scientific institutions.

## STATES AND TERRITORIES OF INDIA

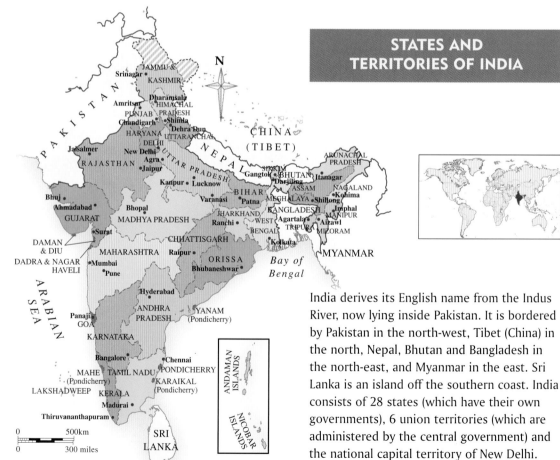

India derives its English name from the Indus River, now lying inside Pakistan. It is bordered by Pakistan in the north-west, Tibet (China) in the north, Nepal, Bhutan and Bangladesh in the north-east, and Myanmar in the east. Sri Lanka is an island off the southern coast. India consists of 28 states (which have their own governments), 6 union territories (which are administered by the central government) and the national capital territory of New Delhi.

New Delhi, the Indian capital city, seen from the air.

## MANY LANGUAGES, MANY RELIGIONS

India's people and cultures are as diverse as its landscapes. Hindi and English are the official languages, but these are two among many. Hindi, with its associated dialects, is the native language of less than half the population, and English is not an Indian language at all. Two-thirds of the population understands Hindi and less than one fifth understands English.

Hinduism is the religion of almost three-quarters of the population. Every town has fine temples, and Hindu festivals are colourful, often involving processions of elaborately costumed figures. About 12 per cent of the population are Muslims and there are also Christians, Sikhs and Buddhists.

In contrast with the ornate architecture and spectacle, however, there are also areas of desperate poverty and severe deprivation. As the Indian economy continues to grow, little by little that poverty will diminish.

## CONTRASTING LANDSCAPES

India is a land of many landscapes. The mighty Himalayan range in the north contains several of the world's highest mountains. It is a region of snow, cold winds and bare rock. In the north-west, the Thar or Great Indian Desert is a dry, inhospitable place, but on the other side of the country, in the north-east, there are tropical rainforests. There are also mangrove forests, swamps and vast expanses of rich farmland.

Together, India, Pakistan and Bangladesh are often called the Indian Subcontinent. The name is doubly appropriate: geographic barriers separate this region from the main part of Asia, making it distinct, and it is also geologically distinct. India was not always attached to Asia. It was once a separate landmass, which drifted northward and collided with southern Asia about 40 million years ago. It was that collision which raised the Himalayas, and India is still thrusting into Asia, so the mountains are still rising.

## KEY DATA

| | |
|---|---|
| Official Name: | Bharat (Hindi) Republic of India (English) |
| Area: | 3,166,414km² |
| Population: | 1,027,015,247 (2001) |
| Official Languages: | Hindi, English |
| Main Cities: | New Delhi (capital), Mumbai, Kolkata, Bangalore, Chennai, Ahmadabad, Pune, Hyderabad, Kanpur, Surat, Jaipur |
| GDP Per Capita: | US$ 2,670* |
| Currency: | Indian rupee (Re; plural Rs); 1 Re = 100 paise |
| Exchange Rate: | 1 US$ = Rs 43.77 1 UK£ = Rs 82.46 |

*(2002) Calculated on Purchasing Power Parity basis.
Sources: *CIA World Factbook, 2004*; World Bank; UN Human Development Report, 2003

# INDIA'S LANDSCAPES

The Himalayan ranges, seen from the city of Shimla, Himachal Pradesh. The world's highest mountains are in the most distant range.

The Earth's outermost solid layer, or crust, consists of rigid sections, or plates, that move in relation to one another. India sits on the Indian Plate, which also includes the floor of part of the surrounding Arabian Sea and Indian Ocean. Geologically, India is distinct from Asia. That fact, and the consequences of the collision between the Indian and Eurasian Plates, give India its physical structure and landscape, and the contrast between northern and southern India.

## THE NORTHERN MOUNTAINS

About 200 million years ago, all the continents were joined together into a single supercontinent called Pangaea. Soon after that, the supercontinent began to break up and that is when India separated from its neighbours and began its slow, northward drift from deep in the southern hemisphere. It crossed the Equator about 60 million years ago and 40 million years ago the Indian Plate collided with the southern margin of the Eurasian Plate. That collision crumpled the rocks to the north, raising the Tibetan Plateau and the Himalayan mountains. The mountains form the first of India's landscapes, and a barrier separating India from Central Asia.

A mountain road in Himachal Pradesh.

## LANDSCAPE FEATURES

0 — 500km
0 — 300 miles

K2
8,611m

N

**PAKISTAN**

Indus

Kullu
Valley

Nanda Devi
7,817m

**CHINA
(TIBET)**

Kanchenjunga Peak
8,586m

**NEPAL**

**BHUTAN**

**H I M A L A Y A S**

**I N D O - G A N G E T I C   P L A I N**

Thar
Desert

Chambal

Ganges

Brahmaputra

**BANGLADESH**

Vindhya Range

Son

Rann of
Kutch

Narmada

Satpura Range

Mahanadi

Sundarbans

Ganges Delta

**MYANMAR**

**DECCAN
PLATEAU**

**Bay of
Bengal**

**A R A B I A N   S E A**

Usmansagar
Lake

Krishna

Tungabhadra

**W E S T E R N   G H A T S**

**E A S T E R N   G H A T S**

Kaveri

Palar

Konkan Coast

Laccadive
Islands

Palk
Strait

Andaman
Islands

Nicobar
Islands

Cape
Comorin

**SRI
LANKA**

*INDIAN OCEAN*

The northernmost is the Great Himalayan Range, where the average elevation is 6,000m. The Great Himalayan Range includes all of the highest mountains. In the west, where India, Pakistan and China meet, this range merges with the Karakoram Range.

To the south of the Great Himalayas, the mountains in the Lesser Himalayan Range are between 1,500m and 5,000m high. The Lesser Himalayan Range extends across northern India, through the states of Himachal Pradesh, Uttar Pradesh, Sikkim and Arunachal Pradesh. The cities of Shimla and Darjiling, where the British once sheltered from the intense summer heat, are located in the Lesser Himalayas.

The Southern or Outer Himalayan Range is the most southerly of the three. These mountains are the Himalayan foothills, averaging 900–1,200m high. In Himachal Pradesh and Uttar Pradesh this range is known as the Siwalik Hills.

Shimla, Himachal Pradesh, is where Europeans formerly retreated during the hottest part of the year. Many of the buildings look British.

### THE HIMALAYAN REGION AND THE FOOTHILLS

The Himalayas are the highest mountains in the world. Everest, the tallest mountain, rising to 8,850m, lies on the border between Nepal and China. K2 is 8,611m tall and lies in a region claimed by India, Pakistan and China. Kanchenjunga, on the India-Nepal border, is 8,586m high, and the peak of Nanda Devi, in India, is 7,817m.

Permanent snow covers the Himalayas above 4,500–6,000m on the southern slopes and above 5,500–6,000m on the northern side. Below the snow line, the northern slopes are mainly forested, but the southern slopes are bare.

There is not one Himalayan range, however, but three parallel ranges. Together they are about 2,400km long and 240–330km wide.

Terraces of rice fields in Kullu Valley, Himachal Pradesh.

## MOUNTAIN VALLEYS

Between the ranges there are high plateaux and fertile valleys, as well as deep gorges cut by the rivers that cascade down the mountainsides. The Kullu Valley in Himachal Pradesh is one of the most beautiful of the Himalayan valleys, stretching southward for 80km on either side of the Beas River, with apple orchards, meadows and rice fields set against the mountain backdrop. The valley has been inhabited for thousands of years. Kulantapith, its ancient Sanskrit name, means 'end of the habitable world'.

## THE INDO-GANGETIC PLAIN

At the southern foot of the Himalayas there is a deep depression where the solid rocks lie below sea level. Over millions of years, this depression has filled with soil washed down from the mountains. Today this region

### CASE STUDY
### THE INDUS VALLEY CIVILIZATION

Patna, then called Pataliputra, was founded in 600 BC and in 321 BC Chandragupta, who established the first Indian empire, made it his capital. He then expanded his empire westward all the way to the Indus. The Indo-Gangetic Plain is the region where Indian civilisation began, although it started long before the reign of Chandragupta. From about 2500 BC, farms in the Indus Valley were raising livestock and growing grains, dates, melons and possibly cotton. They sent their produce to several large cities, including Mohenjo-daro, Harappa, Lothal and Dholavira. Lothal was an important port, trading with Persia and Mesopotamia. The Indus Valley civilisation disappeared around 1700 BC, probably because the climate became much drier and the crops failed.

includes the flood plains of the rivers Indus and Ganges. In the west the mighty Indus, with its tributaries, crosses the Punjab Plain and the Haryana Plain. The rivers Jhelum, Chenab, Ravi, Beas and Sutlej surround the Punjab Plain; the name Punjab is derived from the Sanskrit *pancha ab* meaning 'five rivers'. The Ganges or Ganga, known in Bangladesh as the Padma, rises in an ice cave at the foot of the Gangotri Glacier in the Himalayas. The river then passes through the mountains of Uttaranchal and crosses the plains of Uttar Pradesh, Bihar and West Bengal, ending in a vast delta that merges with the Bay of Bengal.

## RICH LAND

The Indo-Gangetic Plain, comprising the land of the Indus and Ganges river systems, has rich soil watered by seasonal rains and irrigation channels from the rivers. The Plain is the agricultural heartland of India. More than half

Farm workers harvesting wheat by hand in a field on the outskirts of New Delhi. Harvesting this way is slow and very hard work.

of India's rice, wheat and millet are grown in Punjab and Haryana. Patna, the capital city of Bihar and one of the oldest cities in India, gives its name to a variety of long-grained rice that is very popular in the West.

A pilgrim bathing at the source of the Ganges, high in the mountains.

# THE SUNDERBANS

Kolkata (formerly called Calcutta) lies on the Hooghly or Hugli River, the western-most branch of the Ganges, which divides into many streams as it enters the Lower Gangetic Plains of West Bengal. To the south of the city, the Hooghly and Ganges Delta forms an expanse of marshland, mangrove forest and small islands covering 10,000km² and known as the Sunderbans, or 'beautiful forest', one of the most famous features of this region of India. Large parts of the area are protected as nature reserves.

The Sunderbans teems with wildlife. There are saltwater crocodiles, Ganges dolphins, sea turtles and sharks, as well as spotted deer and wild boar. The most famous residents, however, are the Royal Bengal tigers. Tigers swim well and can move freely among the islands.

Woodcutters, fisherfolk and honey collectors also live in the Sunderbans. All of them respect and worship Banbibi, goddess of the beautiful forest, and her husband Dakshin Rai, the supreme ruler of the Sunderbans.

# THE DECCAN

The Vindhya and Satpura Ranges of hills and the Chotar Nagpur Plateau in southern Bihar separate the northern regions of India from the Peninsula. The interior of the Peninsula comprises a series of plateaux averaging 300–750m above sea level and intersected by rivers flowing eastward into the Bay of Bengal. This region of rolling hills is known as the Deccan.

The Deccan is tilted eastward so the land is higher in the west than in the east. It is

Members of the Mowali tribe, gathering honey in the Sunderbans mangrove forest.

bordered by hills, called the Western and Eastern Ghats, which meet at the tip of the Peninsula. Coastal plains surround the Deccan. The western plains contain tidal salt marshes, lagoons and fine, sandy beaches. On the eastern side the plain is wider and very fertile.

The Deccan lies at the geographic and cultural heart of India. The Vindhya and Satpura hills are in Madhya Pradesh State, which stretches across the centre of the country. Its hills are covered with scrub vegetation and during the dry season its plains are scorched by the fierce sun, but it also contains Bandhavgarh and Kanha National Parks, with tigers, mongooses and eagles. Rudyard Kipling's *Jungle Book* stories are set in Kanha National Park. Bhopal, the state capital, is a vibrant, fast-growing city.

On its south-eastern side, Madhya Pradesh adjoins Chhattisgarh, a state founded in November 2000. Chhattisgarh contains one third of India's forests. Its people are predominantly tribal.

ABOVE: A view across the Deccan, which covers much of the interior of India.

BELOW: A small boat carrying passengers and their bicycles passes palm trees lining one of the many waterways in Kerala.

The Kailasanatha Temple at Ellora, Maharashtra, was carved out of the rock face in the eighth century.

# SOUTHERN INDIA

Maharashtra, to the south of Madhya Pradesh, is highly industrialised. Its capital is Mumbai (formerly Bombay), but as well as the petrochemical works and factories, in the hills there are farming villages and market towns. The hills of the Western Ghats are green, and farms on the inland plateau grow cotton and fruits that include oranges, sapodilla and mangoes.

Andhra Pradesh is the largest Indian state. There are beaches along the northern part of the coast and further south the coastal plain is an important rice-growing area. Inland, the plateau is rocky. Hyderabad, the state capital, was founded in 1591 and built to a grid pattern, with streets crossing at right angles. It was once home to wealthy rulers called 'nizams', whose palaces still survive as museums. Outside the museums there are countless bazaars. Today the city has a hi-tech industrial district, called Cyberabad. To the north, a twin city, Secunderabad, has absorbed the expansion of Hyderabad. The nizams controlled Hyderabad from Golconda, a fortified city covering $40km^2$, with palaces, mosques, and gardens on a hill overlooking the city. There were diamond mines nearby, from which came the Kohinoor diamond, the world's most famous jewel. It is now part of the British crown jewels.

A young woman collecting ripe coffee berries on a plantation in Karnataka.

Orissa occupies the eastern side of the thickly wooded Eastern Ghats and the lush, fertile, coastal plain. Inland there is the Simplipal National Park, with tigers, elephants, and many other animals.

To the west of Andhra Pradesh, Karnataka extends to the Western Ghats, where coffee, fruits and spices grow on the fertile hillsides. Tamil Nadu, the southernmost state, is a land of paddy fields and palm forests.

In the west, a region of desert and marshland called Kutch is home to semi-nomadic pastoral communities renowned for their craft products. India and Pakistan fought for Kutch. In 1968 the United Nations (UN) resolved the matter and Kutch became part of India. In 2001 an earthquake caused widespread devastation around the main city of Bhuj.

## CASE STUDY
### PASTORALISTS OF KUTCH

Kutch is in north-western Gujarat, bordering Pakistan in the far north-west of India. Northern Kutch has too dry a climate for growing crops. There is pasture for livestock, however, and the people are pastoralists. They live by tending herds of camels, cattle, buffalo, goats and sheep. The animals graze the pasture and when there is no more food the herders move them to the next area. Herders and livestock follow regular routes from pasture to pasture to take advantage of the seasonal rains, remaining for only a short time at each site. Pastoral people live a semi-nomadic life.

Nomads live in dwellings that can be taken down and carried from place to place. Semi-nomads have more permanent homes. While the men are away tending the livestock, the women, children and old people of Kutch stay at home making the craft goods that are an important source of income.

A goatherd with his animals in the Rann of Kutch, Gujarat.

# CLIMATE

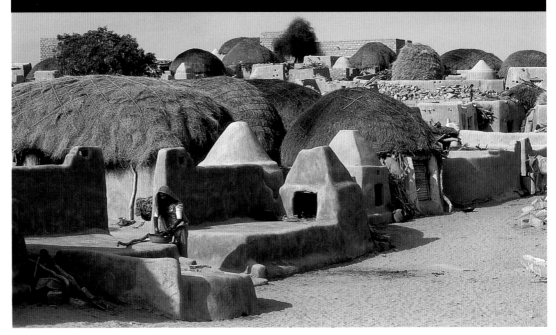

A village near Jaisalmer in the Thar Desert. The dwellings are made from mud with thatched roofs.

Cape Comorin, at the southern tip of India, is at latitude 8° North. The northernmost part of India is at 35° North. The tropic of Cancer, at 23.5° North, divides the country in two. India therefore lies in the tropics and subtropics. Most of the country is affected by the monsoon seasons, but there is also desert and tropical rainforest.

## RAINFALL

In the far north-west, the low-lying Thar or Great Indian Desert lies in Rajasthan. The whole of Rajasthan has a dry climate, with an annual rainfall averaging about 250mm in the east but only 130mm in the desert. Summer temperatures reach 50°C, but they can fall below freezing on nights in winter.

Rainfall increases to the east of Rajasthan. Most of Uttar Pradesh and Madhya Pradesh receive moderate amounts of rain, although they are very hot and dry in early summer. Still further to the east, Bihar, West Bengal, Chhattisgarh and Orissa have a warm, wet climate. Kolkata receives 1,600mm of rain a year, most of it falling during the summer monsoon months, from July to September. Assam, to the east of Bangladesh, is very wet and, with an average

## CLIMATE ZONES

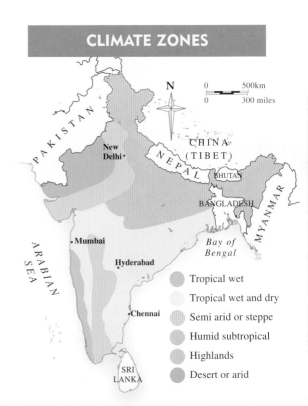

Tropical wet
Tropical wet and dry
Semi arid or steppe
Humid subtropical
Highlands
Desert or arid

10,800mm of rain a year, the town of Cherrapunji is one of the wettest places on Earth. Dhubri, in lowland Assam, receives an average 2,525mm of rain a year – drier than Cherrapunji, but still with 4.5 times the amount of rain that falls on London in the UK.

The central part of the Deccan Plateau is fairly dry. Bangalore, the principal city of Karnataka, receives 900mm of rain a year. Surrounding the dry centre, the main part of the Deccan has a moister, but strongly seasonal climate.

## MONSOON RAINS AND SEASONAL TEMPERATURES

The summer monsoon approaches India from the south-west. The western coastal plain of Maharashtra, Goa and Karnataka has a dry season lasting seven months, but very heavy rainfall during the remainder of the year. Panaji in Goa receives 2,894mm of rain a year on average, but only 145mm falls between the beginning of November and the end of May. The coast of Kerala has a similar climate, but the dry season lasts for only three months. On the eastern coast, the wettest months are October, November and December.

KEY:

Temperature

Rainfall

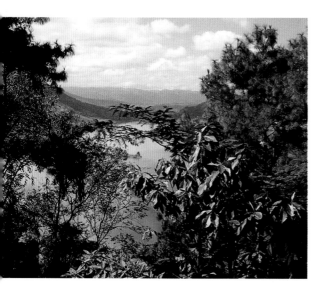

Temperatures in Goa remain at about 26°C throughout the year. This is typical for places on the coast, where the proximity of the ocean moderates the temperature. Places inland experience a much wider range. Winter daytime temperatures in Delhi average 21°C, for example, but in early summer they exceed 40°C.

The landscape around Cherrapunji, Meghalaya, one of the rainiest places on Earth.

# MONSOONS

The word 'monsoon' comes from *mausim*, the Arabic word for season. A monsoon climate is one with a very strong contrast between the seasons. That contrast is linked to a reversal in the direction of the prevailing winds. The change in wind direction that occurs over the Arabian Sea brings dry winters and wet summers to India and most of southern Asia.

In winter, Central Asia becomes very cold. Cold, dense air sinks over the continent producing high surface air pressure. As the air sinks, however, it is compressed by the weight of air above it and this makes its temperature rise. Air spills outward from the high-pressure region, sinks down the Himalayan Ranges, and crosses India as a warm, dry, north-easterly airflow, bringing the dry winter monsoon season.

In summer, the land warms up much more quickly than the ocean and the pressure distribution reverses. Warm air rises over Central Asia, producing low pressure, while pressure remains relatively high over the cooler ocean. Air now flows across the

ocean towards the land, gathering moisture as it does so.

This brings the wet summer monsoon, but the Asian monsoon is much stronger than monsoons elsewhere, because of the Himalayas. These form a barrier preventing the incoming air from moving further north.

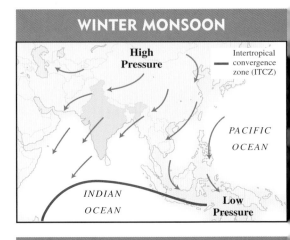

Connaught Place, New Delhi, at dusk, with dark clouds building overhead, promising monsoon rain.

Schoolboys share an umbrella as they walk home in the monsoon rain near Panvel, north of Mumbai.

It is April and in India the ground is parched and the air full of dust. Inland the temperature is rising, soon to pass 32°C during the day, with little relief at night. By May the night-time temperature in Mumbai averages 27°C. This heat is bearable because the air is dry but, as May gives way to June, the humidity starts to rise. Clouds start to appear in the sky. They grow through the day, drifting from east to west, but dissipate by nightfall without bringing rain. Each day the clouds grow bigger and darker.

Then, in late June, the wind strengthens and starts to blow from the south-west. Suddenly the black skies open and rain falls in torrents. People laugh and enjoy their soaking as all the dust is washed from the air and the temperature drops. This is called the 'burst of monsoon'. It is a very abrupt start to the wet summer monsoon. The date on which it happens tells everyone whether the monsoon has arrived on time and the intensity of the storms gives an indication of whether the rain will be sufficient to produce a good harvest – or so heavy that the land will be flooded.

At the same time, the Tibetan Plateau heats up and air rises over it, producing high pressure at high altitude, with air flowing outward from it, and the intertropical convergence zone (ITCZ) moves to its summer position over the mountains. These events combine to generate a high-level easterly wind – a jet stream – that intensifies the movement of air across the Arabian Sea.

The summer monsoon reaches southern India in June, with south-westerly winds blowing at about 45km/h and bringing dark clouds and violent rainstorms. It moves steadily north-westwards, reaching Pakistan around the middle of July. The rains continue through the summer, but from the middle of September they become less intense. The ITCZ moves south for the winter, the easterly jet stream dies, pressure begins to build over Central Asia as the temperature falls, and by the end of December the dry winter monsoon is becoming established.

## WHY THE TRADE WINDS ARE WET WINDS

Blowing on either side of the Equator, the trade winds are the most reliable winds in the world. They blow from the north-east in the northern hemisphere and from the south-east in the southern hemisphere, gathering moisture as they cross the warm, tropical ocean.

The trade winds from both hemispheres meet at the intertropical convergence zone (ITCZ), where air rises, water vapour condenses to form clouds, and there is heavy and frequent rain. The ITCZ moves with the seasons. In the northern summer it lies at about 25° North over Asia, crossing northern India and bringing heavy rain. Kolkata receives 950mm of rain between the beginning of June and the end of August. London receives less than 600mm in the entire year.

A fisherman and his daughters pray for rain standing on the dry bed of Lake Usmansagar in Hyderabad, Andhra Pradesh, emptied by severe drought.

# EXTREMES OF WEATHER
## MONSOON FAILURE

Indian farmers depend on the monsoon rains. If the rains arrive on time and in the usual amounts, the farmers can sow their crops knowing there will be enough water to enable the crops to ripen. If the rains arrive late the crops may have too little time to ripen and the harvest will be poor. If the monsoon fails altogether there will be no harvest at all and people will starve. For example, monsoon failures caused severe famine in 1877–78 and again in 1899–1900. An estimated 5 million people died during the 1877–78 famine. Chennai (formerly Madras) then had a population of 19.4 million, of whom 3.5 million died from hunger and disease. That famine followed an even worse famine in western India lasting from 1868 to 1870 when, in some areas, between one quarter and one third of the population perished. During the 1899–1900 famine, 1.25 million starved and 2 million died from disease.

Between 1965 and 1967, there was a severe drought in Bihar that caused a famine in which 1.5 million people died. However, that was the last occasion on which a failure of the monsoon resulted in tragedy on such a scale. In 1987, India suffered the most widespread drought to hit the country for a century, and in some parts of Gujarat and Rajasthan it was the third year in succession that the monsoon had failed. Relief supplies of food, water and livestock feed were distributed and there was no large-scale famine.

## VIOLENT WEATHER

When the rains arrive they often arrive violently, with torrential storms that can wash away hillsides to cause landslides and mud slides. A short time later, as the deluge draining from the hills fills the tributaries, lowland rivers overflow their banks. That is when floods drive people from their homes and drown farm crops. Too much rain is just as bad as too little.

ABOVE: People travelling along a flooded road in Bihar after heavy monsoon rains caused the Bagmati river to overflow in September 2003.

BELOW: A man retrieves the roof of his home in Nadia village, Assam, after it was blown off during the April 2003 storm.

## THE APRIL 2003 STORM

Even a single storm can cause appalling damage. On the night of 22 April 2003, a storm swept through the Dhubri district of Assam. By the morning at least 45 people had been killed and 4,000 injured, most of them when their thatched houses collapsed onto them or when they were struck by corrugated iron roofs torn from houses by the wind.

That storm gave warning of what lay ahead, as unusually heavy summer rains began to take their toll. In July, Rashid Ahmed, an Assamese farmer, told reporters: 'I've lost my home and agricultural land. Not only mine, around 10 to 12 villages have already been submerged in the floods… We have become beggars now.' In fact, more than 3,000 villages in Assam were under water.

Assam was not the only state to suffer. Large areas of Himachal Pradesh, Bihar, West Bengal, Orissa and Arunachal Pradesh were also inundated, as well as parts of Pakistan and Bangladesh. Millions of people were made homeless and hundreds lost their lives.

Then, as the mud-laden rivers carried sewage through the streets and houses, water-borne diseases began to spread. Cholera, diarrhoea, malaria and other diseases affected hundreds of thousands of people. It was October before the rains eased and the waters began to subside.

# POPULATION

Rush hour on a street crowded with people in Chandni Chowk, New Delhi.

A t midnight on 1 March 2001, the census recorded the population of India as 531,277,078 males and 495,738,169 females – a total of 1,027,015,247, making India the second-most populous country in the world, after China.

## DISTRIBUTION AND STRUCTURE

India's population is not distributed evenly. More people live on each square kilometre of land in the fertile Deccan than in the northern mountains, for example. There are only 13.03 people in every square kilometre of Arunachal Pradesh, and 76.17 per km² in Sikkim, but each square kilometre supports 835.47 people in Bihar and 819.25 in Kerala.

Between 1991 and 2001, the Indian population increased by 21.34 per cent. Indians now comprise one sixth of the world's population, and one third of them are less than 15 years old. India's population will continue to increase as the young reach their reproductive years.

## TOTAL FERTILITY RATE

Women must each bear an average of 2.1 surviving children during the course of their lives if a population is to remain the same size.

The number of children women produce is known as the total fertility rate (TFR). A TFR higher than 2.1 means the population will increase and a TFR below 2.1 means numbers will decrease.

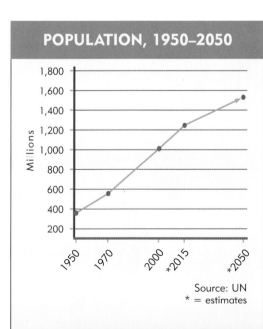

**POPULATION, 1950–2050**

Source: UN
* = estimates

## POPULATION STRUCTURE, 2004

Source: US Census Bureau

## LIFE EXPECTANCY AT BIRTH

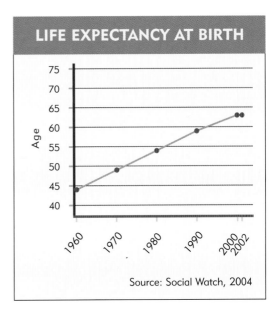

Source: Social Watch, 2004

## UNDER-FIVE MORTALITY RATE

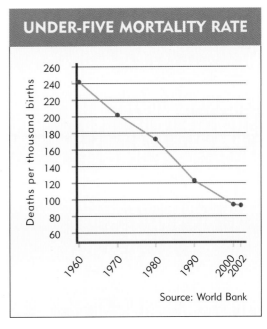

Source: World Bank

## POPULATION DENSITY

Population per km²

over 1000

501-999

251-500

100-250

under 100

In India the TFR has been falling steadily for several years – from 3.11 in 2000 to 2.91 in 2003. If it continues to decrease at this rate it will reach 2.1 in about 2020. It is already at or below 2.1 in 9 states and territories, and between 3.0 and 2.1 in a further 11. The population will continue to increase for some time after 2020, because the number of women will increase as today's children reach adulthood.

## ETHNIC GROUPS AND REGIONS

The Indian constitution recognizes 18 languages, but there are about 180 languages and probably hundreds of dialects. Each region has its own predominant language. The diversity of languages reflects the great variety of Indian peoples.

People in the north are generally tall, slim and light-skinned, while in the south they tend to be darker-skinned and of stockier build. There are people in Orissa who resemble Australian Aborigines, and people with Mongoloid features in the north and north-east.

Haryana and Punjab are the centre of the Sikh religion, but they were also where the Mughal Empire began. The architecture and traditions show the mixture of Muslim and Hindu influences that merge in Sikhism.

Himachal Pradesh, in the hills to the north, is not far from Tibet. Dharamsala is the home of exiled Tibetans and the base of their

ABOVE: Women in Tamil Nadu. These are stocky, dark-skinned southerners who speak Tamil.

BELOW: A family travelling by rickshaw in New Delhi. These are slim, light-skinned northerners who speak Hindi.

spiritual leader, the Dalai Lama. In the snow-covered hills, Buddhist prayer flags and monasteries are dotted among the Hindu temples and monuments. There are also Christian churches and many buildings that look European, for this is the region where Europeans used to retreat from the intense summertime heat of the plains.

Madhya Pradesh and Chhattisgarh are at the heart of Hindu India and have some of India's finest temples. The region was once Muslim, however, and a centre for the Mughals, who ruled India from 1526 to 1707. Before that it was Buddhist. There are fine Buddhist monuments not far from Bhopal in Madhya Pradesh. Chhattisgarh, in the south-east, is densely forested and very different in character. Its people are predominantly tribal.

For centuries, the states occupying the southern part of the Deccan were militarily powerful enough to deter northern invaders.

This helped to isolate Tamil Nadu in the south. Southern Indians look different from northerners, speak what are known as Dravidian languages, and have developed their own Hindu culture. The finest, most ornate Hindu temples are in Tamil Nadu.

## LANGUAGE FAMILIES

More than half the Indian population speaks one or other of 11 Indo-European languages, the most important being Hindi, Urdu, Bengali and Marathi. Hindi and Urdu are written using different scripts, but the languages are very similar and share many words.

Hindi is spoken in and around Delhi. People in Kolkata speak Bengali. In Mumbai they speak Marathi. Tamil is spoken in Chennai. In Kerala people speak Malayalam.

## TRIBES

Tribal people live mainly in the Himalayas, in the hills of the Deccan and in Bihar and West Bengal, but there are some tribes living in most states. Tribes vary in size from about 7.4 million Gonds, living in central India, to fewer than 20 Chaimals in the Andaman Islands. Members of recognised tribes receive special benefits and privileges from the central government.

---

A gypsy woman at a market in Margao, Goa, selling traditional jewellery she has made, similar to the jewellery she is wearing.

## CASE STUDY
### THE ANDAMAN ISLANDERS

Far out in the Bay of Bengal, about 1,000km from the mainland, the 306 Andaman Islands are blanketed in tropical forest, with mangrove forest along the shores and coral reefs offshore. They are also the home of several tribes, including the Jarawas, Great Andamanese, Onges and Sentinelese. The Andaman Islanders are short, dark-skinned and have tight, curly hair. They are related to African peoples.

On 26 December 2004, an undersea earthquake off north-western Indonesia triggered tsunamis that swept across Sri Lanka, south-eastern India and parts of Thailand and Indonesia. The waves swamped all of the Andaman and Nicobar Islands. When the waters subsided, nearly 2,000 Andamanese and Nicobarese were dead and a further 5,500 were missing, presumed dead.

## RELIGION

India is a land of temples and religious festivals. Religion plays a central role in Indian life. Although most people are Hindus, there are also Muslims, Christians, Sikhs and others. India was also the birthplace of Buddhism, although this is now a minority religion in the country.

A holy elephant blessing pilgrims inside the Minakshi Sundareshvara Temple, in Madurai, Tamil Nadu. The elephant's markings symbolise the Hindu god Vishnu.

### HINDUISM

Hinduism is a religion of many deities and colourful rituals. Hinduism emerged about 2000 BC, and today more than 70 per cent of Indians are Hindu. There is no founder or single scriptural authority for Hindu beliefs, but the main tenets of the religion are set out in seven texts called the Vedas. The later Vedas describe a social category of people, called Brahmans, who specialise in interpreting and teaching the texts, and conducting rituals.

## THE CASTE SYSTEM

In India, social status was traditionally inherited and every individual belonged to one of the thousands of occupational groups, or castes. The castes were grouped into four 'varnas'. Brahmans, most of them priests or scholars, held the highest rank. Kshatriyas, rulers and soldiers, came next, followed by Shudras, who were labourers, peasants, craftspeople and domestic servants. Finally the 'untouchables', now called 'Dalits', performed the most menial and degrading tasks. The social hierarchy based on the caste system was developed by the northerners. Indians are now trying hard to break down the barriers it imposes.

In modern India it is illegal to discriminate against someone on the basis of that person's caste, and positive discrimination is practised to help members of the lower castes enter higher education and government employment. Despite this, the caste system still survives.

## RELIGIONS

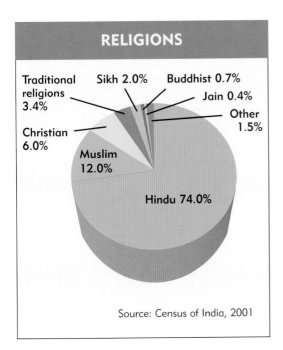

Traditional religions 3.4%

Sikh 2.0%

Buddhist 0.7%

Jain 0.4%

Other 1.5%

Christian 6.0%

Muslim 12.0%

Hindu 74.0%

Source: Census of India, 2001

Pilgrims crossing the courtyard of the Sikh Golden Temple at Amritsar, Punjab, seen from a colonnaded passage.

### ISLAM AND CHRISTIANITY

Islam, which entered India in the seventh and eighth centuries with Arab, Persian and Turkish invaders, recognises only one god, opposes the worship of idols, and its central teachings are set forth in the *Qur'an* and the *Sunnah*. Today about 12 per cent of Indians are Muslim.

A large crowd of Muslims gathered outside a mosque.

Slightly more than 6 per cent of the population is Christian. St Thomas the apostle may have brought Christianity to India in the first century AD, but it spread following the arrival of Vasco da Gama in 1498 and St Francis Xavier in 1542. Many of the Dalits (who are sometimes called 'untouchables') and tribal people are Christians.

### JAINISM, BUDDHISM AND SIKHISM

Jainism was founded in around 599 BC. Jains aim to lead a simple, pure life, avoiding violence to any person and, so far as possible, to any living being. In this way they hope to escape the cycle of birth, death and rebirth.

Founded by Siddartha Gautama, who was born in 566 BC in what is now Nepal, Buddhism spread widely in northern and central India. It regarded all people as equals and Buddhist monasteries became seats of learning and centres of education. By the eighth century AD, however, Buddhist influence was waning in India, but spreading throughout other parts of Asia.

During the fifteenth century, when India was under Muslim rule, the Sikh religion emerged as a reaction against both Islam and Brahmanism. Sikhs believe in one god, and reject the caste system and the worship of idols, but they believe in karma and the cycle of birth and rebirth, which are derived from Hinduism. Sikh men are recognisable by their beards and the turbans they wear to cover their hair, which they must never cut.

# EDUCATION

Before British rule in India, which began early in the nineteenth century, only the sons of high-status families received a formal education. Others were trained for the jobs appropriate to their social position (see caste system box on page 28). The British needed civil servants to help run the country and so they introduced the British educational system, setting up schools modelled on those in England and extending education to the daughters of high-status families.

## LITERACY

Most people remained illiterate, however. The 1951 census, taken several years after British rule ended in 1947, found that only 27 per cent of males and 9 per cent of females were literate, giving an overall literacy rate of 18.3 per cent.

Girls in a class studying outdoors at a rural school in Bodhgaya, Bihar.

**CASE STUDY**
**RURAL SCHOOLS**

The Rural Development Foundation (RDF) is one of many non-governmental organisations that run free schools throughout rural India.

One such school is in Kalleda village in Andhra Pradesh. The RDF and a village committee manage the school for 200 children from kindergarten to age 11. Meals are provided free and the school also supplies uniforms to eliminate caste and class distinctions. Pupils are selected by a lottery to ensure fairness.

Matendla, also in Andhra Pradesh, is considered a backward area. With financial support from the India Literacy Project and the American Telugu Association, the RDF runs Matendla Rural School, which will eventually have 350 pupils up to age 12.

Young men learning to use computers at the Raghabir Nagar Community Centre, New Delhi.

Great advances have been achieved since that time, but the government's goal of compulsory free education for everyone has not yet been attained. Many government schools are very short of basic equipment such as blackboards, books and furniture. Today approximately 75 per cent of males and 55 per cent of females are literate – 65.2 per cent of the total population – although literacy is much higher in urban than in rural areas. There are also geographic differences. In Kerala, almost 90 per cent of people are literate, but fewer than 50 per cent are literate in Bihar.

The Indian government attaches great importance to the improvement of educational provision, and for very practical reasons. Studies have shown that if farmers receive four years of elementary schooling their productivity increases by an average 8.5 per cent, and the introduction in the 1960s of high-yielding 'green revolution' crops and technologies is known to have proceeded faster among educated farmers. Education is a crucial component in the struggle to eliminate hunger. Education also reduces inequalities and increases the share of national income earned by the poorest people. Obviously, as high-technology industries expand, the need for a skilled, educated workforce will continue to grow.

## PRIMARY, MIDDLE AND SECONDARY SCHOOLING

Indian schools are run by the states but financed by central government. Children attend primary school from age 6 to 14. This is free and officially compulsory but, although about 90 per cent of all children enrol at primary school, many do not attend regularly. Only about half of all children enrol at middle school, from 11 to 14. Parents must pay for their children's secondary education up to the age of 18, and only about 20 per cent of young people enrol.

## HIGHER EDUCATION

For the few who go on to higher education, India now has nearly 230 universities and many more agricultural, technical and other colleges. Indian scientists are engaged in world-class research across a wide range of disciplines. For example, India has a space programme and maintains several communications and meteorological satellites.

University students in Chennai.

# URBAN INDIA

India possesses some of the world's greatest, most beautiful and, in places, most crowded cities. Despite the size of its major cities, India is not heavily urbanised, and about 70 per cent of the population live in villages of fewer than 5,000 inhabitants.

The pattern is changing, however. As the economy develops, manufacturing industries and commerce expand. This generates urban jobs that pay wages higher than those people can earn working on farms. At the same time, the modernisation of agriculture makes some farm workers redundant. Displaced or attracted by hopes of a better life, more and more people move into the cities. This happens everywhere and India is no exception, but in India the pace of urbanisation is slow. In 1981, 23.7 per cent of Indians lived in urban areas. This figure increased to 25.7 per cent in 1991 and by 2001 it had reached 27.8 per cent – little more than one quarter of the population.

## CASE STUDY
### SLUMS IN KOLKATA

About 1.5 million people in Kolkata live in slums, like this one beside a canal.

The population of Greater Kolkata grew by more than 40 per cent between 1981 and 2001, from 9.1 million to 13.2 million, and the city has been unable to cope. Of the 4.6 million inhabitants of the city itself, about 1.5 million live in slums. A slum is defined as an area with more than 25 temporary homes, called *katcha* buildings.

In registered slums, called bustees, residents own or rent the ground on which they erect their homes. There may be as many as 500 *katchas* in a bustee. Unregistered slums, which have sprung up along roadsides, beside canals, and on vacant ground, offer no such security. Kolkata has 2,011 bustees and 3,500 unregistered slums.

Three-quarters of the slum population live below the poverty line. Many are unemployed. Others work as rag-pickers, rickshaw-pullers, and casual labourers. Kolkata Municipal Corporation is striving to provide these areas with a clean water supply, sanitation, waste disposal facilities, street lighting, schools and better employment prospects.

## URBAN POPULATION

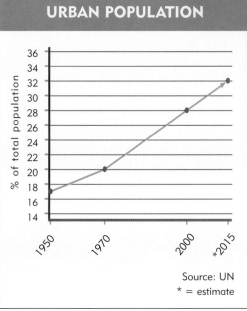

% of total population

36
34
32
30
28
26
24
22
20
18
16
14

1950    1970    2000    *2015

Source: UN
* = estimate

Indian cities are overwhelmed by the growth in traffic and population. Traffic on this street in Old Delhi is gridlocked.

## LIFE IN THE CITY

The new city dwellers maintain close links with their home villages. It is usually a man who moves to the city, often alone but sometimes accompanied by his wife and children. He keeps in touch with his parents, brothers, sisters, uncles, aunts, cousins, nieces and nephews back in the village, visiting when he can and sending them money. If he succeeds in his new life, other family members may follow his lead.

Many of those moving into the cities set up their own businesses making and selling craft goods, running shops, driving taxis, or providing some other service. Not everyone succeeds, however, and many people are in poorly paid jobs, work only intermittently or can find no work at all. The poor live in squalid, overcrowded slums that contrast starkly with the modern apartment blocks and spacious houses of the rich.

Although the rate of urbanisation is slow, the Indian population is so large that this migration has greatly increased the size of the urban population. India's largest city is Greater Mumbai (Bombay), comprising the city of Mumbai and the urban area surrounding it.

The population of Greater Mumbai has doubled in 20 years, from 8.2 million in 1981 to 16.4 million in 2001. Other Indian cities have expanded at a similar rate.

Rapid urban expansion has severely strained city services. Public transport is crowded and traffic jams are common. Cities are struggling to provide adequate sewers, storm drains to carry away rainwater, and a reliable supply of clean water. Education and health services have difficulty coping with the demands made on them.

Brigade Road in the 'electronic city' of Bangalore, Karnataka, where neon signs and bright shop fronts attract passers-by.

# GOVERNMENT

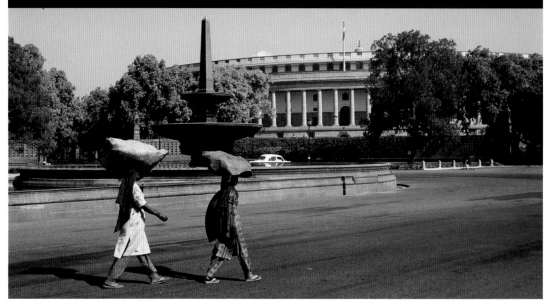

Two women carrying loads on their heads walk past the parliament building in New Delhi.

In 1858 Indian territories formerly controlled by the British East India Company were made part of the British Empire. Most of India was then ruled by the British and Queen Victoria became Empress of India. After a long struggle, India won back its independence in 1947.

India is sometimes described as the world's largest democracy and, in April and May 2004, it held the world's largest election. Nearly 380 million people voted (out of an electorate of 675 million) and polling took place on four separate days as officials moved one million voting machines to locations in different states.

## THE PRESIDENT AND THE PRIME MINISTER

India's president is the head of state. He or she has certain powers, such as declaring states of emergency and calling on the leader of the political party with the greatest parliamentary support to form a government. In practice, the president is rarely able to act except on the advice of the government.

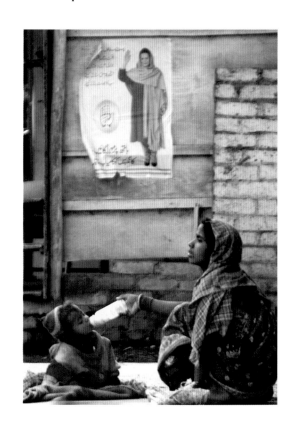

A mother feeds her child in front of an election poster for Sonia Gandhi, leader of the Congress Party, on a street in Lucknow, Uttar Pradesh.

The prime minister heads the government, choosing the members of his or her cabinet from among elected members of parliament. The prime minister, cabinet and junior ministers oversee the running of the country. The judges and courts of law are independent of the government.

## THE HOUSES OF PARLIAMENT

India's legislature, or law-making institution, consists of two houses of parliament. The lower house, called the Lok Sabha or people's assembly, has 542 members elected for five years. Every citizen over 18 years of age is entitled to vote. The upper house, called the Rajya Sabha or council of states, has 250 members. The president appoints 12 of these, choosing individuals who have made distinguished contributions to national life, and the state assemblies elect 238.

On the recommendation of the prime minister, the president appoints the governors of each of the 28 states. The governor is the state equivalent of the national president. Local governments exist at the city, town, district and village level.

## REDRAWING STATE BOUNDARIES

At the time of independence in 1947, India's state boundaries took little account of local cultures and languages. During the 1950s, demands grew for the boundaries to be redrawn on a linguistic basis, so that a single language would predominate in each state. In 1952 Andhra Pradesh, where Telugu is the most widely spoken language, became the first linguistically defined state. In the 1950s and 1960s, several other such states were created, including Tamil Nadu, Kerala and Gujarat, for Tamil, Malayalam and Gujarati speakers respectively.

## CASE STUDY
### THE DIVISION OF PUNJAB

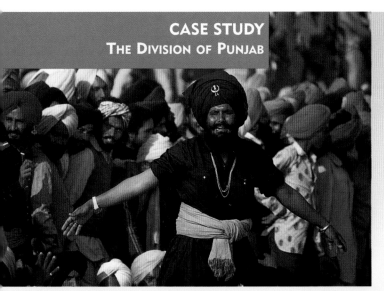

Sikh men, instantly recognisable by their turbans and beards, on a street in Punjab.

Punjab to create what were known as the Himalayan Provinces. These are now called Himachal Pradesh, which became a state in 1966 with its capital at Shimla.

Indian Punjab was further divided in 1966 to separate the region where most people follow the Sikh religion from the predominantly Hindu region. The Sikh region is the modern state of Punjab and the Hindu region is the state of Haryana. Punjabi is the predominant language in Punjab and Hindi in Haryana.

Punjab and Haryana share the same capital, Chandigarh, which was specially built in the 1950s to a design by the Swiss-French architect Le Corbusier. Since the city is the capital of two states and belongs exclusively to neither of them, it is classed as a Union Territory, governed directly by the central government.

The Indian states of Punjab and Haryana were once part of a much larger territory called Punjab. At independence, Punjab was divided into two approximately equal parts, one lying inside India and the other in Pakistan. Territories were then removed from Indian

# KASHMIR

Kashmir, in the far north of India, was once one of the princely states, consisting of Kashmir itself, with its summer capital at Srinagar, Ladakh in the east bordering Tibet, and the district around the winter capital of Jammu in the south-west. The great majority of the people were Muslim, but Hindus and Sikhs formed a majority around Jammu, and Ladakh was predominantly Buddhist.

At independence in 1947, the rulers of all the princely states were allowed to choose whether their territories should become part of India or of Pakistan. Hari Singh, the Hindu Maharajah of Kashmir, hesitated and in October 1947 tribesmen crossed the border from Muslim Pakistan, headed for Srinagar and occupied about 40 per cent of the territory. Faced with the prospect of losing his kingdom, Hari Singh decided that Kashmir should become part of India and he appealed to New Delhi for help. Indian troops were flown to Srinagar and after fierce fighting the tribesmen were forced to retreat.

The dispute was referred to the UN. It negotiated a cease-fire and called for a plebiscite – a vote of the entire population – to decide Kashmir's future.

Srinagar, the summer capital of Jammu and Kashmir, is a city of lakes, gardens, and beautiful wooden buildings.

In 1949 a cease-fire line was drawn, placing 38 per cent of Kashmir on the Pakistan side and 62 per cent on the Indian side. The plebiscite has still not been held and both India and Pakistan continue to lay claim to the entire region.

## SPECIAL STATUS FOR KASHMIR

In order to persuade the people of both parts of Kashmir to join India, Article 370 of the Indian Constitution gives Kashmir special status, allowing it to make its own laws and run its own affairs in all matters except for defence, foreign affairs and communications.

The status of Kashmir remains undecided. Some people accuse India of persistently interfering in Kashmiri politics, thus undermining the state's autonomy, and of promoting the interests of the Hindu minority at the expense of the Muslim majority. Certain Kashmiri groups want union with Pakistan while others would like Kashmir to become an independent country. Within India there are Hindu groups, including the Bharitaya Janata Party, which maintain that Kashmir is an

Wagah, on the border between Indian and Pakistani Kashmir. Every day, Pakistani rangers (right) try to beat the Indian border police in a race to lower their flags and close the border.

integral part of India and is not entitled to special status. The organisations calling for Kashmiri independence boycotted the elections that were held in 1996.

Pakistan continues to assert its claim on Kashmir and supports militant groups fighting inside Kashmir. India is thus compelled to maintain large military and paramilitary forces in the area. Kashmir is the scene of a low-level war that, from time to time, escalates into a direct confrontation between India and Pakistan. Thousands of lives have been lost and most Hindus have left the worst affected areas.

### CASE STUDY
#### WAR AND NUCLEAR CONFRONTATION

Congress Party supporters marching through Kolkata to urge the government to take action against Pakistan over Kashmir.

Fighting over Kashmir has broken out between India and Pakistan in 1947, 1965 and 1999. The 1947 war began when tribal fighters crossed into Kashmir from Pakistan. In 1965 Pakistan-backed guerrillas infiltrated Kashmir, leading to skirmishes with Indian troops and retaliation from Pakistan that escalated into war. In 1999, conflict began when Pakistani troops in civilian dress infiltrated north of the city of Kargil, establishing positions from which they could shell various targets and from which they were driven mainly by air attacks.

Since 1998 there have been fears that nuclear weapons might be used in future wars. India conducted an underground nuclear test in 1974 and, on 11 May 1998, tested three nuclear devices in Rajasthan. The newly elected Bharatiya Janata Party government then declared India to be a nuclear-weapon power. Between 28 and 30 May, Pakistan responded by carrying out six nuclear weapon tests.

# FOREIGN RELATIONS

India became independent of Britain in a spirit of good will on both sides. France also held territories in India and control of these was also handed over peacefully. Portugal, however, refused to relinquish its territories of Goa, now a state, and the towns of Damão (now Daman) and Diu, which are now union territories. In December 1961 India took these territories by force.

India is a republic, but remains a member of the Commonwealth, an international organisation headed by the British Queen.

## NON-ALIGNED MOVEMENT

Jawaharlal Nehru, India's first prime minister, was determined that India should play an active international role. He sought to place India in a position where it could mediate between the Western and Communist blocs by pursuing a policy of 'non-alignment'. India encouraged other Asian nations to unite around their common interests and, in 1955, the Indian government took part in a conference of 29 Asian and African nations held in Bandung, Indonesia. The Bandung Conference established the non-aligned group of nations of which India is still a prominent member.

India, then a British territory, was a founding member of the United Nations in 1945 and actively supports the UN. India has contributed more than 55,000 military and civilian police to 35 UN peacekeeping operations, as well as troops, paramedics and observers to UN forces in many parts of the world. It has also chaired several UN commissions set up to implement cease-fire agreements. The Indian Army has helped to clear mines in Rwanda, Mozambique, Somalia, Angola and Cambodia.

## CHINA, THE USSR AND THE USA

Nehru tried but failed to establish warm relations with China, and in 1962 the two countries fought a war in which India was defeated. This led India to seek stronger ties with the Soviet Union, largely to counterbalance the ties Pakistan was developing with China and the USA. Later, as the Cold War continued, US relations with China improved and the USA became the major provider of aid and supplier of arms to Pakistan, driving India even closer to the Soviet Union. When Soviet forces occupied Afghanistan in the 1980s, the USA supported the Afghan resistance, based in Pakistan.

Today, the USA is India's biggest trading partner and US support for Pakistan has weakened following the end of the Cold War. Relations between India and the USA remain strained though, due to India's possession of nuclear weapons and its refusal to sign the Nuclear Non-Proliferation Treaty (because of the failure of the five original signatories to destroy their own nuclear stockpiles).

An Indian UN patrol near Ghajar village on the border between Israel and South Lebanon.

Tibetan Buddhist monks, refugees at Dharamsala, Himachal Pradesh.

India recognised the Communist government in China in 1949 and sought friendly relations. But it condemned the Chinese invasion of Tibet in 1950 and said it would defend the border states of Nepal, Bhutan and Sikkim. In 1959 the Chinese suppressed a Tibetan uprising. India did not condemn the suppression, but gave shelter to the Dalai Lama and large numbers of Tibetan refugees.

Chinese troops crossed into north-eastern India in August 1959. China asserted territorial claims in the region and consultations failed to resolve the issue. In 1962 China invaded and Chinese forces advanced quickly, overrunning Indian positions, but then withdrew. There were further clashes in 1967, but China did not intervene in the 1971 Indo-Pakistan war.

Former Indian prime minister Vajpayee with Chinese prime minister Zhu Rongji in New Delhi.

# AGRICULTURE AND FORESTRY

Farm workers winnowing rice – sorting the grain from the chaff – in Tamil Nadu.

India is modernising its economy. Manufacturing and service industries provide an increasing proportion of the total number of jobs. Nevertheless, most Indians continue to live in villages and rural areas, and agriculture remains by far the most important national industry. Two-thirds of all Indians work on the land, either on farms or in forests.

Between them, agriculture and forestry generate approximately 25 per cent of India's GDP (gross domestic product), yet they account for 65 per cent of the workforce. Almost every part of India is farmed, and land under permanent crop cultivation accounts for over 57 per cent of the country's total land area. Areas set aside as wildlife refuges, the Thar Desert, beaches and steep, rocky, mountain slopes together occupy about 16 per cent of the land area, forests 23 per cent, pasture and meadows almost 4 per cent, and urban and built-up areas, such as roads, 0.2 per cent.

## CROPS

Wheat and rice are the most important staple foods – those that provide the bulk of what people eat. Wheat is grown on the western

AGRICULTURE

Millets
Wheat
Rice

## DIET (% OF CALORIES DERIVED FROM VARIOUS FOODS)

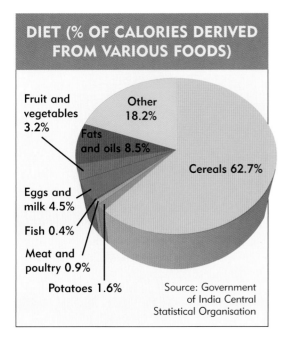

Fruit and vegetables 3.2%
Fats and oils 8.5%
Other 18.2%
Cereals 62.7%
Eggs and milk 4.5%
Fish 0.4%
Meat and poultry 0.9%
Potatoes 1.6%

Source: Government of India Central Statistical Organisation

### THE GREEN REVOLUTION AND RISING YIELDS

India benefited greatly from the introduction of new varieties of wheat and rice, along with increased use of fertiliser and better irrigation, during the so-called 'green revolution' of the 1960s and yields continue to rise. Average wheat yields between 1995 and 2000 were 40 per cent higher than between 1971 and 1980. Rice yields rose by 65 per cent during the same period.

The increase in output means that India now produces enough food for its population. According to the Food and Agriculture Organisation (FAO) of the United Nations, Indians now receive 112 per cent of the recommended minimum number of calories per day. This is an average figure, however, and conceals the fact that while some sections of society eat very well there are others who often go hungry.

In all countries where agriculture is the most important industry, wages are low and people are poor. India is no exception. More than 50 per cent of the average household income is spent on food. In the UK, this figure is 20 per cent.

side of the Deccan Plateau and across northern India, extending well into the Himalayan foothills. Rice is grown throughout the country.

Sorghum and millets are also grown widely. These produce seeds that are ground into flour that can be cooked to make a kind of porridge or baked as unleavened bread. Some varieties of sorghum have a sweet-tasting stem, rather like sugar cane.

In addition to cereal crops, Indian farmers grow sugar cane, tea and coffee. Sugar cane grows on lower ground over much of the country. Tea grows best in the hills of north-eastern India, especially in Assam, which produces more than half of all Indian tea, and the hills around Darjiling, West Bengal. Tea is also grown in south-western India, in Karnataka and Kerala. Coffee is grown mainly in Karnataka.

Picking tea on a plantation in the hills near Darjiling, West Bengal.

## HOUSEHOLD EXPENDITURE (% OF TOTAL INCOME)

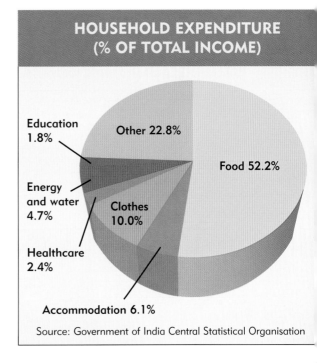

Education 1.8%
Other 22.8%
Energy and water 4.7%
Clothes 10.0%
Food 52.2%
Healthcare 2.4%
Accommodation 6.1%

Source: Government of India Central Statistical Organisation

# IRRIGATION

Indian farmers rely on the monsoon rains that supply approximately three-quarters of the country's annual rainfall. The monsoon is unreliable, however, and the water it delivers falls so rapidly that a great deal runs away and is lost before plant roots can absorb it. Irrigation provides water when it is needed, rather than when the climate delivers it, and making water available at the right time can dramatically increase yields.

Two-thirds of Indian farmland is watered only by the rain, and one third is irrigated. Artificial reservoirs held behind dams provide water for all uses, and more dams are being planned and built. About five-sixths of the water held in these reservoirs is used for crop irrigation. Despite the rises in output achieved in recent decades, the average yield of Indian cereal crops is still less than half that in China and the USA. Expanding the area of irrigated land and improving farming techniques could raise Indian yields to these levels.

## TRADITIONAL IRRIGATION

Traditionally, irrigation water is lifted from a well or river by means of either a bucket-and-pole device or a wheel. The bucket-and-pole, known in India as a *denkli* or *paecottah*, comprises a long, tapering pole mounted on a crossbeam. A bucket hangs from one end and the other end is counterweighted. A worker pulls on a rope to lower the bucket into the well. When the bucket is full, releasing the rope allows it to rise.

The wheel, called a *harat*, is mounted on a horizontal axis. It carries buckets that fill at the bottom and empty their contents into irrigation channels at the top. Mechanical pumps are tending to replace these ancient devices.

Surplus irrigation water must be allowed to drain away. If it accumulates the land may

---

Irrigation on farm land in Punjab. Water pumped from the ground flows through a system of channels that take it to the fields.

Hindus drink milk and eat butter and other dairy products, but they will not permit cattle to be killed for food and they will not eat beef. Cows are allowed to walk through the streets. When a family buys a new cow, its legs are ritually washed and it is welcomed into the home with a religious ceremony.

Cows are sacred because they are so useful. They provide milk, so they resemble human mothers. Oxen, the males, pull the plough and other farm implements, helping the farmer to produce food for his family. Cow dung fertilises the soil.

The religious significance is deeper, however. Krishna, an incarnation of the god Vishnu, was a cowherd and played his flute to

Cows holding up the rush-hour traffic on a main road in Varanasi, Uttar Pradesh.

the cows in his charge. In one story, a cow called Kamadhenu gave milk to Vishnu. Every Hindu god has an animal companion and Shiva, the destroyer of evil, rides on a bull called Nandhi.

become waterlogged and the evaporation of surface water will leave behind dissolved salts that slowly poison the land – a process called salinisation. Large areas of Indian cropland have suffered from waterlogging and salinisation.

## LIVESTOCK

As well as plant crops, Indian farmers also raise livestock. Each year, India produces about 400 million chickens, 94 million water buffalo, more than a million camels, 123 million goats, 58 million sheep, 16 million pigs and a staggering 219 million cattle. Water buffalo, oxen and camels are working animals. The other species are raised for food, wool and skins. The chickens lay approximately 1.8 million tonnes of eggs each year and the cattle yield 22 million tonnes of milk.

Goatherds driving their animals along a road in Rajasthan. The animals are unperturbed by the passing trucks.

# FORESTS

About 2,000 years ago, forests covered 85 per cent of India. Many human communities lived in the forests and found all of their food and materials there. People managed the forests even then, by planting trees they found useful and clearing land to grow crops.

The situation changed during the nineteenth and twentieth centuries, when forests were cleared to provide farmland for more profitable crops. The rapid expansion of the railways in the late nineteenth century consumed huge amounts of wood to make sleepers and to build stations. Satellite images show that today only 23 per cent of India is forested. Large areas of forest are still being lost, mainly because of illegal cutting by local communities to provide land for raising livestock. At present, Indian forests produce approximately 303 million m$^3$ of wood a year, of which 279 million m$^3$ is fuelwood.

## SOCIAL FORESTRY

Approximately one third of the Indian population – some 360 million people – live in or close to the forests. Nearly one fifth of those – 68 million people – are classed as tribal or indigenous peoples. These are among the poorest members of Indian society. Consequently, the forested areas have the highest density of tribal areas, and more than 60 per cent of the people living in the forests of Jharkhand,

The forests of Madhya Pradesh, seen from the highest point in the Satpura Range of hills.

West Bengal, Madhya Pradesh, Chhattisgarh and Orissa are below the poverty line. These are the people whose way of life depends on the forests.

Beginning with the Indian Forest Act of 1878, forests have been brought under the control of the central government. Local

The home of a tribal family living in the forested hills of Meghalaya, in north-eastern India.

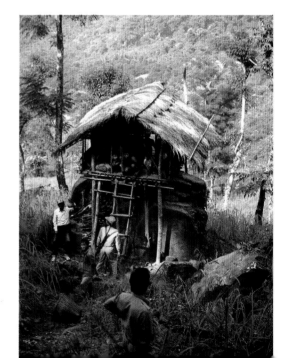

communities found their rights to the produce of the forests, which they had enjoyed throughout their history, were redefined as privileges and then taken away altogether.

In recent years, the Indian government has recognised this problem. In 1976 it launched the Social Forestry Programme (SFP) with the aim of satisfying the needs of local communities without compromising the supply of industrial timber. Most SFP projects were successful. Between 1950 and 1979, forests were being planted at an average rate of 0.11 million hectares a year. The rate rose to 1.3 million hectares a year between 1980 and 1989.

There were problems, however. In particular, the SFP suffered from an industrial bias. Villagers needed trees to supply fruit, fuel and fodder for their livestock. However, most plantations grew eucalyptus, which grows fast and produces high-quality timber for the construction industry, but no edible leaves or fruit.

**FORESTS**

● Forest area

Students watering seedlings in a tree nursery in the Rishi Valley, Andhra Pradesh.

## JOINT FOREST MANAGEMENT

Social forestry is now being replaced by Joint Forest Management (JFM). Its aim is to restore and regenerate up to 50 million hectares of degraded land. Forest projects are organised by local groups of 10 to 100 households, with the support of the state forest department. JFM does not transfer the ownership of the forests, most of which belong to the state, but it allows local communities to control access to the forests and to decide how they should be managed. The forests supply the needs of the villagers without harming the wild plants and animals.

# INDUSTRY

The nuclear power station at Elephant Island, Mumbai. India has six nuclear power stations and is increasing its use of nuclear power.

Although agriculture is the biggest industry in India, its importance is decreasing as the economy modernises. The founders of independent India determined that the country would develop an advanced industrial economy. They planned the energy, transport, communications and financial structures that would support rapid industrialisation. Industrialisation would provide jobs and reduce poverty.

In 1950 agriculture, forestry and fisheries generated 59 per cent of GDP and manufacturing – mainly jute and cotton textiles – 10 per cent. Today agriculture generates only 25 per cent of GDP, industry also generates 25 per cent, and the service sector generates 50 per cent.

This change has raised the standard of living, but it will be some time before Indian living standards match those in the West. Although over 75 per cent of Indian urban homes have electric light and almost 64 per cent have an indoor toilet, access to these facilities is much lower in rural areas where the majority of Indians live. Nationally, just over 40 per cent of homes have electric light and less than 24 per cent have an indoor toilet.

## RESOURCES

India possesses the natural resources needed for industrialisation. It has reserves of iron ore, chromite, lead, zinc, copper and bauxite (aluminium ore). Chromite is the principal chromium ore and chromium is used to make high-quality steel. To power its smelters,

foundries and factories, India has reserves comprising more than 84 billion tonnes of coal, nearly 440 billion $m^3$ of natural gas, and 4.8 billion barrels of oil.

Fossil fuels generate 80 per cent of the country's electricity, with hydroelectric plants

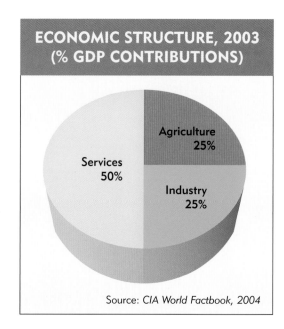

### ECONOMIC STRUCTURE, 2003 (% GDP CONTRIBUTIONS)

Agriculture 25%

Services 50%

Industry 25%

Source: *CIA World Factbook, 2004*

providing about 16 per cent. There is also a small contribution from nuclear power. In 2004 India had six nuclear power stations, with a total of ten working reactors, and six more reactors were under construction.

# NEW INDUSTRIES

Although traditional industries, such as textile manufacture, continue to provide a large amount of employment, they are no longer the most valuable industries. Whereas textiles contribute about Rs100 billion to the economy each year, the manufacture of motor vehicles contributes Rs120 billion and the chemical industry, making synthetic fibres, agrochemicals, drugs and medicines, paints, cosmetics and soaps, contributes Rs237 billion.

These industries pay higher wages than the older industries. Workers in the agrochemical industry earn more than double the national average wage, and those working in oil refineries earn 3.5 times the average. Even so, wages are still low enough to attract foreign companies and many western organisations have relocated their call centres to India (see page 51). Rising prosperity, at least among high-paid workers, is stimulating the demand for leisure services and so this sector is also expanding.

Workers packing medicines at a pharmaceuticals factory in Mumbai.

# THE BALANCE OF TRADE

Despite the economic progress India is making, the value of the country's imports continues to exceed that of its exports – by Rs359 billion in 2001–02. At present, jewellery and cut and polished diamonds provide 20 per cent of India's export earnings, ready-made cotton garments 9 per cent, and leather goods 4 per cent. Oil is the biggest import.

## MAJOR TRADING PARTNERS (% OF VALUE), 2003

**EXPORTS**

USA 22.5%
Others 54.4%
UK 5.1%
UAE 5.1%
Hong Kong 4.5%
Germany 4.3%
China 4.1%

**IMPORTS**

USA 7.1%
Belgium 6.7%
China 4.6%
Singapore 4.6%
UK 4.6%
Others 72.4%

Source: CIA World Factbook, 2004

# TRADITIONAL INDUSTRIES

Modern industries pay high wages, but some traditional industries employ far more workers, many of them highly skilled, producing goods that are exported all over the world. For example, approximately 20 million people work in the textile industry.

## LUXURY FABRICS

Varanasi, on the banks of the Ganges in Uttar Pradesh, is one of the world's oldest cities and is sacred to both Hindus and Buddhists. It is also a centre of textile production. For more than 2,000 years, weavers at Varanasi have been producing the finest cotton cloth, and since the sixteenth century they have been incorporating gold and silver threads to make luxurious brocades. Their richest cloths were traditionally made for royalty and exported to Tibetan monasteries, but the weavers also produce fine silk saris and scarves. Craft workers at Agra, also in Uttar Pradesh, use gold thread and beads to make *zardosi* – fabrics embroidered with elaborate designs.

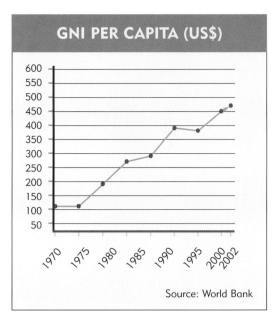

**GNI PER CAPITA (US$)**

Source: World Bank

## TRIBAL CRAFTS

Craft products provide a useful income for many tribal people. The techniques and designs are part of tribal culture, but the beauty and vivid colours of the products ensure a ready demand for them.

Metal ornaments, especially those made from brass, are exported, as are items made from cane and carved wood. Craft workers also produce hand-knotted carpets.

Weaving silk to make saris on a handloom in the old city of Varanasi, Uttar Pradesh.

This tribal woman in Sikkim is weaving a carpet with a traditional design.

Loading coal onto a truck at an opencast mine in Bihar.

Reform of the Indian economy, which began in the late 1970s, is based on reducing state control. As part of this process, Indian coal mines are to be privatised. Trade unions fear that privatisation will lead to lower wages and a return to poorer conditions.

India is also the world's largest producer of mica, used mainly for electrical insulation and to make windows for industrial furnaces, and a major producer of a range of other minerals. These resources are distributed throughout India and employ about 700,000 workers. The minerals industry contributes only about 2.5 per cent of GDP, however, although it accounts for 10 to 11 per cent of industrial GDP. When cut diamonds are excluded, mineral exports amount to only 3.1 per cent of total exports.

## COAL AND MINERALS – THE EXTRACTIVE INDUSTRIES

Not all of the traditional industries are so colourful. India has more than 500 coal mines, located in Assam, Bihar, West Bengal, Madhya Pradesh, Uttar Pradesh, Maharashtra, Orissa and Andhra Pradesh. India is the world's third-largest producer of hard coal (as opposed to brown coal or lignite), after the USA and China. Power stations are the biggest customers for Indian coal.

The coal industry has been state owned since the early 1970s, when it was nationalised. Over 90 per cent of all coal production is controlled by Coal India Ltd (CIL), the state operating company.

Since nationalisation, investment has increased and working conditions, which were once dangerous, have improved. CIL employs about 643,000 workers and since 1974–75 annual expenditure on welfare services and housing for miners has increased from Rs200 million to Rs11 billion.

**MINERALS AND ENERGY**

**Energy Resources**
≈≈ HEP
⬛ Coal
🛢 Oil

**Mineral Resources**
- Fe Iron ore
- Mn Manganese
- Mi Mica
- C Chromite
- Zn Zinc
- M Magnesite
- G Gypsum
- Pb Lead
- Cu Copper
- Al Bauxite
- S Salt

49

# MODERN INDUSTRIES

## IRON AND STEEL

The iron and steel industry is important: as well as supplying the domestic market, it earns valuable foreign exchange through exports. Domestically, iron and steel are made into a wide range of machines and machine tools that are used in many industries. India also exports machinery.

## THE MOTOR INDUSTRY

Indian factories have been making cars, motor cycles and commercial vehicles since the 1940s and the motor industry is now very large. There are nearly 3,800 factories employing almost 400,000 people. In 2001–02 the industry produced more than 163,500 cars and multi-utility vehicles, nearly 29,000 commercial vehicles and more than one million motor cycles and three-wheelers. Many of these were exported, mainly to Latin America and Eastern Europe.

Foreign manufacturers, including General Motors, Ford, Honda and Daewoo, have set up plants in India, but there are also Indian companies. Hindustan Motors, with an annual turnover of more than one billion rupees, is the oldest, and produced the first Indian car in 1942. The biggest company, Maruti Udyog Ltd (MUL), was established in 1981 as a joint enterprise between the Indian government and Suzuki of Japan.

## ELECTRONICS

The electronics industry is expanding rapidly and now supplies almost all the computer disk drives, dot matrix printers, line printers, plotters, monitors and keyboards used in India. Computers, TV sets, microwave cookers and washing machines are also manufactured in India and, as well as domestic goods, the industry produces electronic components for communications.

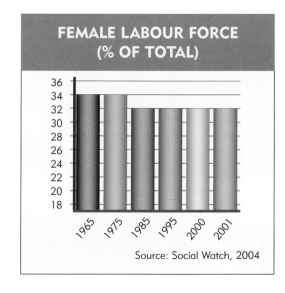

**FEMALE LABOUR FORCE (% OF TOTAL)**

Source: Social Watch, 2004

---

The end of the production line at the Hindustan Motors Thiruvallir Plant, Kerala.

LANCER

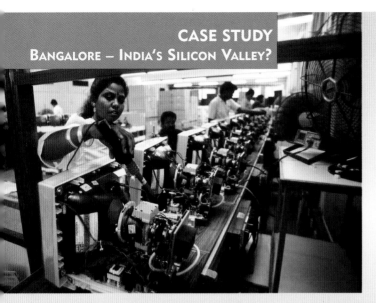

Workers assembling computer monitors at a factory near Bangalore, Karnataka.

Much of the electronics industry is centred in and around the city of Bangalore, in Karnataka – India's fastest-growing city with a population of more than 4 million. The city has a high concentration of electronics companies that manufacture hardware to established designs. There is no Indian company manufacturing semiconductors – the 'chips' that lie at the heart of every electronic device; these must be imported.

Many of the Bangalore enterprises are engaged in supplying software services. When an organisation needs a computer programme to perform particular functions, a Bangalore company will be able to write and develop it. In years to come, the industry may begin to compete globally with entirely new electronic products.

## CALL CENTRES

Telephone enquiries from customers needing advice about products or services, or help in using them, are usually directed to specialist call centres. These now handle a very wide variety of enquires and they also sell products by telephone – 'telemarketing'.

Call centres are major employers, which means their wage bills are high. In recent years, a growing number of Western companies have relocated their call centres to India, where wages are lower and operating costs are 40 per cent cheaper. By March 2004, European and American companies had recruited 170,000 call centre workers in India and the number is expected to reach 1.1 million by 2008. Many Indian call centres are in Bangalore.

All Indian call centre workers are university graduates who speak good English. They earn the equivalent of about £40 a week. A call centre worker in the UK would be paid about £250 a week, but the Indian salary is about the same as that of a newly qualified doctor and twice a teacher's salary.

These workers at a call centre in Bangalore, Karnataka may well be talking to customers in the UK.

# TRANSPORT AND COMMUNICATIONS

A plane at Bangalore airport belonging to Air Deccan, India's first budget airline.

## RAIL

India has the second-largest rail network in the world, after China. More than 63,000km of track link 6,856 train stations, and every day Indian Railways (IR) runs about 8,700 passenger and 5,700 freight trains, carrying more than a million tonnes of freight and about 14 million passengers.

Indian Railways is a state-owned company that manages the entire network, together with the train stations and services such as cleaning and catering. The network is divided geographically into 16 zones. In addition, the Kolkata Metro, India's first underground service, is owned and operated by IR but is not included in any of the zones, and the Konkan Railway is a separate but incorporated operation. It runs for 760km along the Konkan Coast from Mumbai to Thiruvananthapuram in southern Kerala, across 2,137 bridges and 140 rivers, and through 83km of tunnel. It is the country's fastest service, travelling at 160km/h.

Of the total track, 45,000km is broad gauge, 14,800km metre gauge and 3,300km narrow gauge. In effect this means there are three separate networks. The company has begun to replace the metre- and narrow-gauge track so that the entire network will eventually consist of broad-gauge track. The plan is then to bring in faster trains, running at up to 160km/h.

## ROAD, SEA AND AIR

Major cities are linked by 52,000km of well-maintained national highways. State highways cover 129,000km and there are also many minor roads, some no more than dirt tracks, which criss-cross the country. Many people now travel by private car, but there is also an extensive bus and coach network linking the cities and travelling into more remote regions.

Passenger ferries link some coastal cities, such as Kolkata and Chennai, and sea-going

Passengers leaving a crowded commuter train at Mumbai station.

## TRANSPORT

Main road
Railway
International airport

0 ——— 500km
0 ——— 300 miles

liners operate passenger services to the Andaman and Lakshadweep Islands.

Air India provides air links between India and the outside world. Inside the country, Indian Airlines flies between 7 international and more than 88 internal airports. Vayudoot is an airline operating turboprop aircraft: it plans to expand to reach more than 140 airports, serving the remotest parts of India.

## TELEPHONES, TV, RADIO AND NEWSPAPERS

Telephone lines do not reach some of the very remote villages, but the service is growing and most will be connected by about 2007.

Private telephones are uncommon and most telephones are for public use. Very few people have mobile phones (see table below) but they are gradually becoming more widespread.

More people have a TV than have a telephone, and the number is increasing with the spread of satellite and cable TV. There are about 83 TV sets for every 1,000 people. Radio reaches a much bigger audience. There are 120 radios for every 1,000 people.

Indian daily newspapers have a combined circulation of about 19 million. This is the same as the daily circulation in the UK, and is small for such a populous country. As well as the national dailies, there are many regional and local newspapers.

## TELECOMMUNICATIONS DATA (PER 1,000 PEOPLE)

| | |
|---|---|
| Mainline Phones | 40 |
| Mobile Phones | 12 |
| Internet Users | 16 |

Source: World Bank

## PERSONAL COMPUTERS (PER 1,000 PEOPLE)

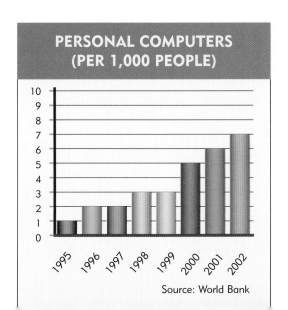

Source: World Bank

## TELEVISION SETS (PER 1,000 PEOPLE)

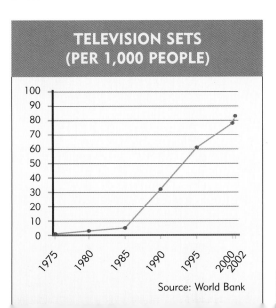

Source: World Bank

# THE ENVIRONMENT, LEISURE AND TOURISM

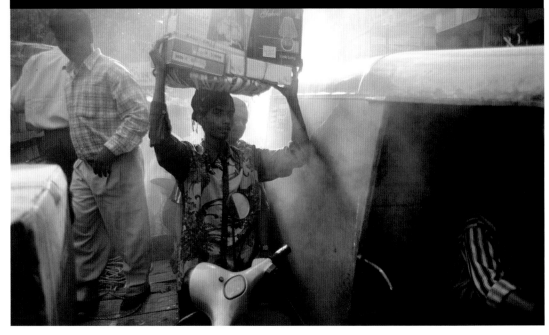

A porter is enveloped in clouds of exhaust fumes and unable to move through a traffic jam in New Delhi.

## THE ENVIRONMENT

India has more than 20 cities with over one million inhabitants. New Delhi, Mumbai, Chennai and Kolkata are among the most polluted cities in the world, and more people die prematurely due to air pollution in India than in any other country.

A 1976 amendment to the Indian constitution committed the government to safeguarding the quality of the environment. This commitment was reinforced by the Environment Protection Act, passed in 1986.

In New Delhi it is illegal to drive any vehicle that is more than 15 years old and in New Delhi, Mumbai, Chennai and Kolkata emission standards for private cars and commercial vehicles now match those in the European Union. Buses that run on compressed natural gas (CNG) are replacing New Delhi's diesel buses. CNG is a much cleaner fuel.

Half of the energy used in India comes from burning coal, which produces pollution. The government is encouraging the development of renewable energy resources. It favours solar energy, principally as a means of supplying electricity to small villages in remote rural areas. In these situations, solar cells are more economical than conventional sources of power. India also hopes to generate more power from large-scale hydroelectric schemes.

Students cleaning the solar panels that heat water for their school in the Rishi Valley, Andhra Pradesh.

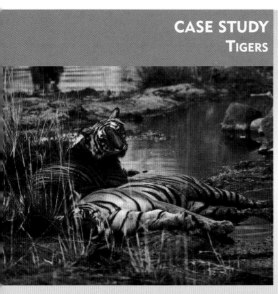

Bengal tigers resting by a stream in Ranthambhore National Park, Rajasthan.

India contains 60 per cent of the world's tigers and, until 1970, it was legal to hunt them for their skins. Hunters killed more than 3,000 tigers during the 1950s and early 1960s.

When people realised that the number of tigers was decreasing alarmingly, the authorities took action. Project Tiger was launched on 1 April 1973, in Corbett National Park in Uttar Pradesh. The Corbett National Park is still the most famous tiger reserve, but there are 66 protected areas for tigers. Despite the conservation efforts, however, there are now probably no more than about 3,000 tigers in the wild in India.

India has 65 national parks and more than 300 wildlife sanctuaries listed with the United Nations. Many of these are open to visitors and they are major tourist attractions.

## AFFECTED ENVIRONMENTS

Soil degradation, due to erosion, overgrazing, waterlogging and salinisation, is serious in some areas. Improved farming methods and more efficient irrigation are being encouraged as a way of restoring damaged soil and preventing further loss.

Water pollution is serious in some cities, where untreated sewage and industrial effluents contaminate rivers. Although increasing numbers of people have access to a piped water supply, 2 per cent of the population obtains drinking water from a river or canal.

Wildlife is also threatened, particularly through loss of habitat – for example, where forests have been cut down to make way for farmland. India contains 172 species of animal considered globally threatened by the IUCN (International Union for Nature Conservation) – 2.9 per cent of the world's threatened species. These include Jenkin's shrew, the Namdapha flying squirrel, Salim Ali's fruit bat and Wroughton's free-tailed bat, all of which are found only in India. The Asian elephant, Indian rhinoceros and Ganges River dolphin are also threatened, as well as the Bengal tiger (see case study above).

The worst industrial accident the world has ever seen occurred on the night of 2–3 December 1984, at Bhopal, Madhya Pradesh, where a subsidiary of the US company Union Carbide was manufacturing pesticides.

The incident began when water accidentally flowed into a storage tank containing methyl isocyanate (MIC), triggering a reaction that released extremely poisonous MIC gas. At about 11.30 pm workers felt their eyes were smarting and told their supervisor, but the leak continued for 2 hours. MIC gas is heavier than air. It settled to the ground and flowed downwind for about 8km through a residential area where people were sleeping. At least 3,000 people were fatally poisoned and hundreds of thousands were injured. Many of the survivors were left with chronic illnesses affecting their eyes, muscles, respiratory system, digestion and nervous system.

# LEISURE AND TOURISM

Baga Beach, Goa, offers a wide expanse of soft, white sand.

As India grows more prosperous, increasing numbers of Indians can afford to take holidays. Many of them choose to travel abroad. In 2003, 4.5 million Indians enjoyed holidays abroad and that number is increasing. The USA is their most popular destination, but the tourist boards of many other countries are opening offices in India in an attempt to attract a share of this business. Indian visitors are popular because it is felt that many are more interested in food and shopping than in sightseeing, and so they tend to spend more than tourists from other countries.

Most Indians, however, prefer to take their vacations in their own country. In 2003, 300 million Indian citizens visited tourist areas. Surprisingly, perhaps, the majority of domestic tourists live in rural areas rather than the

## CASE STUDY
### BOLLYWOOD

India has a thriving movie industry, nicknamed 'Bollywood', producing up to 1,000 feature films a year. Films featuring mythology, melodrama, romance, action and suspense, with songs and dances, are known as 'Bombay talkies' or 'masala movies' (masala is a mixture of spices). India is perhaps the only country in the world where home-produced movies attract much bigger audiences than imported US movies. The films are filled with popular heroes and heroines, song-and-dance routines, well-choreographed fights and simple storylines.

These people in Sikkim are queuing to buy tickets to see the latest Bollywood movie.

cities. Many are visiting relatives or friends and visit tourist attractions in the same area. These 'social travellers' account for 59 per cent of domestic tourists. Pilgrims and those visiting religious sites account for a further 14 per cent. So many travellers are now Indian that the major hotels are redirecting their advertising and promotion to offer attractive packages to domestic visitors.

## FOREIGN VISITORS

Foreign holidaymakers have also discovered India, which is now rated one of the world's most popular tourist destinations. In 2003, India welcomed 2.8 million overseas visitors, from Europe, North America, Asia, Africa, Australia and New Zealand. About 30 per cent of them were from the UK and the USA.

## POPULAR ATTRACTIONS

It is now easier than ever before for tourists to explore India. The network of national highways provides well-maintained roads, and airfares have fallen. International airlines have increased the frequency of flights to India – although at peak times demand sometimes outstrips supply.

Kerala is the most popular tourist region for Indians. Situated between the Arabian Sea and the Western Ghats, the state has wide, palm-fringed beaches, boat trips along extensive waterways, and wildlife reserves. It is also famed for its version of Ayurvedic medical treatments, which use therapies based on herbal medicines.

Most foreign tourists visit the Taj Mahal, one of the most famous buildings in the world. It is in Agra, Uttar Pradesh, the former Moghul capital of India and only 204km from New Delhi, the modern capital.

Goa is a popular area with both Indian and Western holidaymakers. It has buildings that reflect its past as a Portuguese colony, including whitewashed churches and grand cathedrals. There are also coconut plantations, rice fields and Hindu temples, as well as beaches stretching for more than 100km along the Konkan coast.

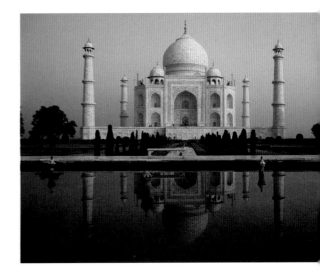

The Taj Mahal at Agra, Uttar Pradesh attracts large numbers of tourists.

Tourism is now a major industry in India. In 2003 its turnover was nearly Rs400 million. Although India has captured only about 0.4 per cent of the global tourism market, tourism already provides almost 20 million jobs and, after textiles and diamonds, it is the third-highest earner of foreign exchange. Economists predict that the industry will continue to expand rapidly.

# LOOKING AHEAD

India is classed as a developing country, but it is changing rapidly. Already it is a major industrial nation, exporting manufactured goods to many parts of the world. Within the next few years Europeans and Americans may well be driving cars made in India and then, following the Japanese model, cars assembled locally in Indian-owned factories. India will also be exporting computers and other electronic devices, taking part of the market now held by other Asian countries.

Because of its size, however, Indian development is likely to be regional rather than being concentrated in a few areas. By 2050, India may be a leading economic power as well as the world's most populous nation, while retaining its vibrant cultural diversity.

# GLOSSARY

**Ayurvedic**  Describes a system of medicine widely practised in India, based on the theory that the body is controlled by three forces and that illnesses are due to imbalances between them. Therapies, mainly herbal medicines, aim to restore the balance.

**Burst of monsoon**  The abrupt onset of the wet summer south-westerly monsoon, which begins with a violent rainstorm that ends the long drought.

**Caste system**  A Hindu social structure that divides people into occupational groups. Individuals are born into a caste. Traditionally it was impossible for anyone to move from one caste to another and there was little informal social contact between members of different castes.

**Cold War**  The rivalry between capitalist and socialist economic and political systems that emerged after World War II and developed into a military stand-off between members of the North Atlantic Treaty Organisation (NATO) and the Soviet-led Warsaw Pact. It ended with the political collapse of the Soviet Union.

**Dalit**  The people formerly classed as untouchable in the Hindu caste system. Dalit, their own name for themselves, means 'depressed'.

**Deccan**  Southern; most often applied to the Deccan Plateau.

**Desert**  Any region where the annual rainfall is less than the amount of water that could evaporate during the same period. The amount of rainfall below which deserts form varies according to the average temperature, but less than 25mm of rain a year will produce desert almost anywhere.

**Flood plain**  Level land on either side of a river that is periodically inundated when the river overflows its banks or that is immersed as meanders in the river advance across the area.

**GDP (Gross Domestic Product)**  A measure of national income. The value of all the goods and services produced within a country over a stated period (usually one year), charged at market prices and including taxes and subsidies (treated as negative taxes).

**Ghats**  Steps; the Western and Eastern Ghats are ranges of mountains that run some distance inland and parallel to the western and eastern coasts of India respectively.

**GNI (Gross National Income)**  The monetary value of goods and services produced by a country plus any earnings from overseas in a single year. It used to be called Gross National Product (GNP).

**Green revolution**  A programme of agricultural reform and modernisation, based on the introduction of new varieties of wheat and rice and the technologies to grow them, that was devised and coordinated by the Food and Agriculture Organisation (FAO) of the UN in the 1960s.

**Humidity**  The amount of water vapour (not liquid droplets or ice crystals such as cloud or fog) present in the air.

**ITCZ (Intertropical Convergence Zone)**  A belt around the Earth where the trade winds from the northern and southern hemispheres meet.

**Jet stream**  A ribbon of wind blowing at 105–500km/h at an altitude of 7.5–12km.

**Lok Sabha**  The House of the People; the lower house of the Indian parliament.

**Mangrove**  A tree that grows in coastal mud below the high-tide line. There are many species. Mangroves trap mud and thereby extend the coastline.

**Monsoon**  A season of extreme weather characterised by the direction of the prevailing wind. India has a monsoon climate comprising a dry, north-easterly, winter monsoon and a wet, south-westerly, summer monsoon.

**Paddy**  A field of rice that is flooded for part of the growing season, or rice grown in such a field.

**Pangaea**  A supercontinent that came into being about 240 million years ago, when all the world's continents united. Pangaea lasted for about 40 million years before starting to break up.

**Pastoralist**  A person who earns a living by herding livestock, driving them from one area of seasonal pasture to another. Pastoralists are either nomads or have permanent homes but spend part of each year away from home, tending their animals.

**Plebiscite**  A referendum, or vote of all the people on a single issue.

**Princely states**  More than 560 regions of the Indian subcontinent that were outside direct British control prior to independence. Each had its own ruler, but the ruling princes had to remain on good terms with the British. After independence the princely states were incorporated into either India or Pakistan.

**Rajya Sabha** The Council of State; the upper house of the Indian parliament.

**Salinisation** The accumulation of mineral salts near the soil surface, usually linked to waterlogging and caused by poor irrigation. Salinisation can render the soil sterile.

**Snow line** The elevation on a mountainside above which snow lies throughout the year.

**Supercontinent** A continent formed by the union of smaller continents.

**Total fertility rate (TFR)** The average number of surviving babies born to each woman in the course of her life. A population with a TFR of 2.1 will remain the same size. A TFR higher than 2.1 means the population will increase and a TFR of less than 2.1 means the population will decrease in size.

**Trade wind** The wind that blows in the tropics, from the north-east in the northern hemisphere and from the south-east in the southern hemisphere. Trade winds blow very constantly along the same track; 'trade' is an old word for 'track'.

**Tribal people** Members of communities that did not accept the caste system at the time when Hinduism was established. They live in the more remote forest and mountain regions away from the mainstream of society. They are also known as Adivasi, meaning 'aboriginals'.

**Tsunami** An ocean wave, generally caused by an undersea earthquake or volcano. Tsunamis spread out from their source in all directions, and can travel across oceans at up to 400km/h and reach heights of 10m.

**Tube well** A well made by driving a tube vertically downward into the ground until it reaches to below the water table and the lower part fills with water. Also called a driven well.

**Waterlogging** The accumulation of water below ground that occurs in hot climates where water evaporates rapidly from the soil surface and farmers apply increasing amounts of irrigation water to compensate, but fail to provide drainage to remove surplus water. Crop plants suffer and eventually die when water saturates the soil around their roots. Waterlogging can also lead to salinisation.

# FURTHER INFORMATION

## BOOKS TO READ:

*Eyewitness Travel Guides: India* by Abha Narain Lamba (Dorling Kindersley, 2002) A guide to every part of India, with many geographical and historical details.

*Modern India* by Joti Sekhon. (McGraw-Hill Higher Education, 2000) A short description of India, its history, religions, society and politics.

*The Age of Kali* by William Dalrymple (Harper Collins, 1998) Very informative and easy to read.

*A History of India* by John Keay (Harper Collins, 2001) A very good, comprehensive book about the country.

*The Rough Guide to India* by David Abram, Devdan Sen, Nicki Edwards, Mike Ford and Beth Wooldridge. (Rough Guides, 5th edn. 2003) A detailed guide with much historical information.

*A Traveller's History of India* by Sinharaja Tammita-Delgoda (Cassell & Co., 3rd edn. 2002) A brief, highly readable history of India.

## WEBSITES:

Washington State University – Ancient India: The Land and its Peoples
www.wsu.edu/~dee/ANCINDIA/LAND.HTM

A Gateway to Districts of India on the Web
http://districts.nic.in/

India Community Forestry Profile
www.forestsandcommunities.org/Country_Profiles/india.html

India – Geography
http://countrystudies.us/india/27.htm

India Image: A Gateway for Government of India
http://indiaimage.nic.in/

India – Tribes
http://countrystudies.us/india/70.htm

Population in India
www.indianchild.com/population_of_india.htm

CIA World Factbook
www.cia.gov/cia/publications/factbook/geos/in.html

# INDEX

Numbers shown in **bold** refer to pages with maps, graphic illustrations or photographs.

agriculture *(see also crops, farming)* 13, 32, **40–45**, **46**
Andaman Islands 27, 53
Andhra Pradesh **8**, 16, 17, 30, **45**
  drought **22**
  government 35
  industry 49
Arunachal Pradesh **8**, **11**, 23, 24
Assam **8**, 18, 19, **22–23**, 41, 49

Bangalore **8**, **9**, 19, **33**, **51**, **52**
Bay of Bengal 13, 14
Bhopal **8**, 15, 55
Bihar **8**, 13, 14, 18, 22, **23**, 24, 27, **30**, 31, **49**
Bollywood movie industry **56**
British rule **11**, 30, 34

call centres 47, **51**
caste system 28, 29, 30, 58
Chandragupta 12
Chennai **8**, **9**, 27
  environment 54
  famine 22
  transport 52
  university **31**
Chhattisgarh **8**, 15, 18, 27, 44
civilisation, ancient **8**, 12
coal *(see also energy, resources)* 46, **49**, 54
Commonwealth 38
communications 46, 50, 52, **53**
computers 50, **51**, **53**, 57
cotton 12, 16, 46, 47
crops *(see also agriculture, farming)* 31, 40
  forest clearance 44
  Indus valley 12
  irrigation **42**
  rainfall 22

da Gama, Vasco 29
Dalai Lama 27, 39
Darjiling 11, **41**
Deccan Plateau **11**, 14–**15**
  agriculture 41
  climate 19

culture 27
population 24
tribal people 27
democracy 34
desert 9, 17, **18**, 40, 58
diamonds 16, 47, 49, 57
drought **22**

economy *(see also GDP, GNI)*,
  agriculture 40
  future 57
  growth 9
  industry 46, 47, 49
  tourism 57
  urbanisation 32
education *(see also school)* 30–31, 33
electricity *(see also energy)* 54, 46
electronics industry 50, **51**, 57
elephants 17, **28**, 55, **61**
employment 32, 33, 46, 47
energy *(see also electricity)* 46, **49**, **54**
exports *(see also economy, trade)* **47**, 48, 50, 57

factories *(see also industry)* 16, 46, **47**, 50, 57
farmers and farming *(see also agriculture, crops)* 9, **13**, 16, 17, **40**
  agriculture 41
  education 31
  environment 55
  floods 23
  forest clearance 44
  irrigation 42
  livestock 43
  monsoon 22, 23
floods 21, **22–23**
forests and forestry 40, **44**, **45**, 46, 55

Gandhi, Sonia **34**
Ganges river **8**, **11**, **13**, 14, 48
Gautama, Siddhartha 29
GDP (gross domestic product) *(see also economy)* **9**, 58
  agriculture 40
  industry **46**, 49
Ghats **11**, 15, 16, 17, 57, 58

GNI (gross national income) *(see also economy)* **48**
Goa **8**, 19, **27**, 38, **56**, 57
government 34–39, 45, 50, 54
green revolution 31, 41, 58
Gujarat **8**, **17**, 22, 35

Haryana **8**, 13, 26, 35
Himachal Pradesh **8**, **10–11**, **12**, 23, 26, 35, **39**
Himalayan mountains 9, **10–11**
  agriculture 41
  monsoon 20
  tribal people 27
Hyderabad **8**, **9**, 16, **19**, **22**

independence 34, 35, 37, 38
India Literacy Project 30
Indus river **8**, 12, 13
industry *(see also factories, manufacturing)* **8**, **46–47**, **48**, 49, 50, 51
  agriculture 40, 41
  Bhopal accident 55
  education 31
  movies 57
  timber 45
  tourists 57
  urbanisation 32
irrigation 13, 41, **42**, 55

Karnataka **8**, **16**, 17, 19, 33, 41, 51
Kashmir **8**, **36–37**
Kerala **8**, 15, 19, 24, 27, 31, 35, 41, **50**, 52, 57
Kipling, Rudyard 15
Kolkata **8**, **9**, 14
  climate 18
  government **37**
  inhabitants 54
  language 27
  rainfall 21
  slums **32**
  transport 52

languages **9**, 26, 27, 35
life expectancy **25**
literacy 30, 31
Madhya Pradesh **8**, 15, 16
  climate 18

elephants **61**
forests **44**
industry 49
temples 27
Maharashtra **8**, **16**, 19, 49
mangrove forest 9, **14**, 27, 58
manufacturing *(see also factories, industry)* 46, 47, 50, 57
Meghalaya **8**, **19**, 44
monsoons 18, 19, **20–21**, 22, 23, 42, 58
motor car industry 47, **50**, 57
Mughal Empire 26, 27
Mumbai **6**, **8**, **9**
  climate **19**
  industry 16, **47**
  inhabitants 54
  language 27
  monsoon 21
  nuclear power **46**
  train **52**
  urbanisation 33

national parks 15, 17, **55**
Nehru, Jawaharlal 38
New Delhi **8**, **9**
  climate **19**
  education **31**
  farming **13**
  inhabitants 54
  monsoon **20**
  parliament **34**
  people 26

rush hour **24**
traffic **33**, **54**

oil industry 46, 47, **49**
Orissa 6, **8**, 17, 18, 23, 26, 44, 49

phones **53**
pollution 54, 55
population 8, **9**
  education 30–31
  ethnic groups 26, 27–33
  increase **24**, **25**
  language 27
  religion 28, 29
  urbanisation 32–33
poverty 9, 32, 44, 46
Punjab **8**, 13, **29**, **35**, **42**

rainfall 18, **19**, 21, 22, 42
Rajasthan **6–7**, **8**, 18, 22, 37, **43**, **55**
religions 9, 26, **28–29**, **43**, 57
resources *(see also coal, oil)* 46, **49**
rice **12**, 13, 16, **40**
  agriculture 41
  tourists 57
Rural Development Foundation 30

salinisation 43, 55
school *(see also education)* 30, 31, 32
Sikkim **8**, **11**, **24**, **39**, **48**, **56**

slums **32**, 33
space programme 31

Taj Mahal **6**, **57**
Tamil Nadu **8**, **26**, 27, **28**, 35, **40**
temples 9, **16**, 27, **28**, **29**
  tourists 57
Thar Desert 9, **11**, **18**, 40
tigers 14, 15, 17, **55**
tourism 55, 56–57
transport 33, 44, 46, **52–53**, 57
tribal people 27, **44**, **48**, 58

United Nations (UN) 17, 36, **38**, 41, 55
Uttaranchal **8**, 13
Uttar Pradesh **8**, 10, 18
  industry **48**, 49
  Taj Mahal **6**, **57**
  tigers **55**

Varanasi **8**, **43**, **48**

war 37, 38, 39
West Bengal **8**, 13, 14, 18, 23, 27, **41**, 44, 49
wildlife 14, 40, 55, 57

Domestic working elephants walking through a river at Satpura, Madhya Pradesh.